simply genius

FOOD52

simply genius

recipes for beginners,
busy cooks & curious people

kristen miglore

photography by james ransom
illustrations by eliana rodgers

TEN SPEED PRESS
California | New York

contents

speedy, sensible workday breakfasts

weekend fun breakfasts

lofty buttermilk pancakes 34
from dana velden

glorious croissant bread pudding 40
from shilpa uskokovic

3 more ways to riff like shilpa 42

joe's famous "fried" bacon 43
from joe's bakery

chickpea soccata with tomatoes & kale 44
from ria dolly barbosa

iced café de olla 49
from rick martinez

slow-baked broccoli frittata 50
from andrew feinberg

3 more ways to frittata 54
from louisa shafia, lauryn chun & lukas volger

caramelized cream smashed potatoes 55
from aki kamozawa & h. alexander talbot

scrambled red shakshuka 56
from sami tamimi & tara wigley

MINIS: 2 BRUNCH BELLS & WHISTLES

red fruit salad 60
from stacey rivera

limonada de cacahuate 61
from roberto santibañez

good things to make ahead for lunches (& dinners & snacks) all week

soy sauce eggs 64
from momofuku

frijoles negros de la olla 68
from gonzalo guzmán

crispy black-eyed pea hummus 72
from jerrelle guy

3 more second lives for beans 73
from gonzalo guzmán, tejal rao, ara zada & kate leahy

lentils folded into yogurt, spinach & basil 75
from peter miller

buttermilk-marinated roast chicken (aka chicken for tomorrow) 76
from samin nosrat

chiles toreados 79
from roberto santibañez

slow-roasted chicken with extra-crisp skin (aka chicken for today) 82
from lindsay maitland hunt

winter slaw with farro 84
from deb perelman

farro & olive salad 86
from heidi swanson

shockingly easy no-knead focaccia 88
from sarah jampel

mayonnaise d'avocat 91
from dr. jessica b. harris

MINIS: 2 SNACKS FOR WHILE YOU WAIT

shishito-style green peppers 94
from michele humes

deviled egg spread 95
from todd richards

hands-off dinners for when you want to start cooking, then do other things

slow-roasted salmon (or other fish) 152
from sally schneider

3 more ways to season your salmon 156
from marc matsumoto, ben mims & eric kim

cold salmon & potatoes with herby yogurt & paprika oil 157
from emma laperruque

sheet-pan gnocchi with chili crisp & baby bok choy 158
from hetty mckinnon

pepperoni pizza gnocchi 160
from ali slagle

one-pot coconut water abc soup 162
from yi jun loh

coconut water nuoc cham 165
from andrea nguyen

chicken fennel quinoa porridge 166
from aaron hutcherson

crispy chicken thighs 171
from christopher hirsheimer & melissa hamilton

pork shoulder ragù (aka the instant dinner party) 172
from andy ward & jenny rosenstrach

shortcut polenta 175
from maria speck

MINIS: 2 QUICK, HAPPY SAUCES

fresh tomato sauce 178
from jacques pépin

crunchy radish pico 179
from pati jinich

mix & match sides (or dinner, if you eat enough of them)

insalata estiva, insalata invernale 182
from rose gray & ruth rogers

3 more smart salad dressings 187
from anjali prasertong, annada rathi & diane morgan

white wine–simmered collard greens with oven-dried tomatoes 188
from bryant terry

quick-sautéed stems 191
from bryant terry

sheet-pan roasted mushrooms & greens 192
from millie peartree

roasted butternut squash & red onion with tahini & za'atar 196
from yotam ottolenghi & sami tamimi

baked sweet potatoes with maple crème fraîche 200
from nik sharma

roasted potatoes with paprika mayo 204
from molly yeh

MINIS: 2 SUPERFAST GREEN SIDES

honey-sautéed spinach 208
from yi jun loh

skillet scallions 209
from edna lewis

desserts anyone can make

the basics

ROADMAP TO ALL THE GENIUS TIPS

foreword

by amanda hesser

When Kristen began dreaming up this book, she envisioned a compendium that taught people how to cook. But not how to cook in the way that most books do. She had no interest in creating yet another manual jammed with French-influenced whipping and poaching and searing that often produces more dirty dishes than empowered home cooks.

An instruction book wasn't Kristen's style anyway. She is an obsessively practical, honest, and busy home cook, who's going to show you how to do the things that matter—like how to revive leftover rice (page 134) and how to cook oatmeal without a sticky pot left behind (page 18). She'll tell you what to do if things go wrong with your fried eggs or ragù. And she'll be your friend annotating a set of her favorite recipes, giving you photos and illustrations and tips from her experience.

Because isn't this what we all need in the kitchen? Yes—we all need a Kristen who shares the nuggets of friendly wisdom and savvy that make good cooking great, who tirelessly tracks down the best recipes, and who laughs with us when our pancakes look like a Rorschach inkblot.

Kristen has been writing Genius Recipes, our most popular column, since 2011. She now does YouTube videos and a podcast, and has published two books, *Genius Recipes* and *Genius Desserts*. Over this past decade, as she crisscrossed the vast, congested recipe landscape in search of transformative yet accessible recipes, she began cataloging the techniques and sleights of hand that some cooks use to distinguish their recipes. Like slow-roasting frittata so it's more tender (page 50). Knowing the best tricks to achieve never-gritty salad greens (page 185). Or crisping and caramelizing potatoes, not in butter or oil, but cream (page 55).

The Genius series has thrived all these years because Kristen has empathy for home cooks. She knows what it means to be time-strapped, lacking tools, and desperate for original ideas. She, too, wants inspiring food. She's not aiming to impress you with snazzy, cutting-edge restaurant dishes; she's here to delight you with approachable recipes that stand above all others. A genius recipe is one that changes the way you cook and one that you'll want to cook for the rest of your life—like Magic 15-Second Creamy Scrambled Eggs (page 10) and Honey-Sautéed Spinach (page 208).

Kristen, in her own sleight of hand, has managed to assemble more than one hundred spectacular recipes, along with revelatory tips, variations, and techniques that will teach you how to cook—just not in the ways everyone else does. I plan to keep this book on my countertop, a reminder that cooking is a miracle of tiny actions and discoveries.

introduction

I was standing in the kitchen with my almost-two-year-old on a wooden chair next to me, passing sticky measuring spoons and cups back and forth, littering the counter and floor with oats and splats of maple syrup. While I tested Jenné Claiborne's Tahini Pistachio Granola (page 22) in a big bowl with proper measurements, my daughter was mixing her own little freestyle batch on the side, happily eating her work along the way.

I slid the sheet pan into the oven. We wiped the counter, singing the clean up, clean up song. The kitchen air sweetened with toasting oats and sesame. Fifteen minutes later, we were blowing on clumps of warm granola and turning off the oven. My daughter hadn't had a chance to get bored and wander away; I woke up every day that week thinking of the next bowl I'd get to eat.

When I started working on this book in 2018, long before she was born, it was meant for beginners. I pictured the recipes I'd hand to my someday-child to get her hooked on cooking—to show how much she could do in the kitchen with little effort, time, and gear.

But I didn't realize how much I would end up needing those recipes myself over the next three years—through the stupor of early parenthood and the strain of the pandemic, then a move across the country to start again. The late-night dinner my husband and I could silently form, stirring torn pita through eggs and brown butter, knowing we might be up again in three hours, was Leah Koenig's Fatoot Samneh (page 13) with heavy squeezes of honey. The green side that could be on our plates in ten minutes while we both tried to parent a toddler and work from home was Michele Humes's Shishito-Style Green Peppers (page 94). The other breakfast I could tag-team with my daughter any morning she asked for it was Samantha Seneviratne's Cocoa Almond Oatmeal (page 18). These are the recipes that fill this book: the ones that can bend around whatever life hands you, and make it better.

So whether you're brand new to cooking or just looking for ways to make more good food with little time, what I hope you get out of this book most of all is this: a hundred or so recipes that provide outsize happiness for what they ask of you, from lofty pancakes (page 34) to the juiciest roast chicken (page 76) to maybe the best sweet potatoes of your life (page 200).

If I've done my job right, they'll also point to a flash of insight that you can take with you the next time, whether you follow the recipe to a T or go your own way. Flashes like: You definitely don't need to soak or skim dried beans, or pay much attention to them at all—they'll be both creamier and more hands-free with Nopalito chef and owner Gonzalo Guzmán's rule-breaking method (page 71). Ottolenghi cofounder Sami Tamimi grew up in Palestine not worrying about perfectly poached eggs in his shakshuka—and you don't need to either (page 56). *New York Times* food reporter Priya Krishna's family always steams rice in the microwave (page 105), which, sidenote, makes it really easy to finally clean the microwave. (And so many more.)

You'll see that the recipes are riddled with extra helpful visuals and tips in an effort to re-create holistically one of the most rewarding experiences in life and the best way to learn to cook: hanging out in someone's kitchen watching them chop and stir, taste and adjust. Because even though I wrote down a recipe for my grandmother's biscuits and egg gravy, I wish I'd spent even more time at her elbow while she was alive, taking pictures and nagging her with questions (she would have secretly loved it, I think). With only a list of ingredients and steps and no hand to hold, it never comes together quite right.

This book tries to fill those gaps with the intel I've gathered from the geniuses behind these dishes, from my own misfires and happy accidents, and from Food52 community members who generously share their own discoveries any time I ask if there are better ways to slice a bell pepper or drop potatoes into a pot of boiling water without inviting danger (there always are—page 56 and page 164).

Which brings me to the last thing I hope you take away from this book, as I have in a decade or so of testing recipes from cookbook authors and chefs, writing about them in the Genius Recipes cookbooks and column on Food52, and overanalyzing along the way: a firm conviction that if someone is telling you *the one right way* to cook something, you don't have to believe them. It might be *their right way,* but it isn't the only one. In these pages you'll find the proof: in the soft-scrambled eggs that take 15 seconds instead of 15 minutes (page 10), the salad dressings you don't have to stress about breaking (page 113), the chocolate chip cookies you can make right now, not in an hour when the butter's soft (page 212).

The recipes that follow are the ones that defied what I thought I knew about cooking and, most importantly, slid easily into my life—even when I had a baby strapped to my body, then a toddler stealing my measuring spoons, and in empty kitchens upended by boxes and Bubble Wrap. They brought me and my family joy in times we needed it most. With my deepest thanks to the geniuses who created them, I hope they do the same for you.

when this book can help

My goal in writing this book was to make everything as intuitive and supportive as possible, so you can dive in on any page with success (see more on how the recipes are written to be helpful on page 6). But I do want you to know about a few different ways to find the recipes that will be most useful and delicious for you, any moment you need them.

how to find the recipes you want

BY PRACTICAL NEED: If you look at the table of contents, you'll see that chapters are grouped by the most important needs we face as busy home cooks—things like speedy workday breakfasts, make-ahead lunches, and shareable desserts that don't require expensive equipment or a degree in pastry making. Did you notice that there are three dinner chapters? These are the practical, comforting recipes that we never seem to have enough of—from the quickest meals that fall almost fully formed from the pantry to the set-it-and-forget-it types that cook themselves while you take care of other business or sit down with a beer.

Every chapter is roughly ordered by how much time you'll need to make the recipe—although even the more time-consuming ones can fit into your life if they sound good to you. Some take time but hardly any work, like Von Diaz's Tembleque on page 228 or Shilpa Uskokovic's Glorious Croissant Bread Pudding on page 40. And the handful with longer ingredient lists or instructions can be cooked entirely (or almost entirely) the day before you want to serve them (like Sami Tamimi & Tara Wigley's Scrambled Red Shakshuka on page 56 and Andy Ward & Jenny Rosenstrach's Pork Shoulder Ragù on page 172). And I promise I won't ask you to do extra work—or spend more time or money—for a recipe that won't feed you well and make you very happy.

BY INGREDIENT OR DIET: I know that sometimes you're just in the mood for chicken or suddenly need a vegan brunch recipe, so you can find handy categories like ingredient and dietary need in the index on page 269.

BY MEAL: Sometimes the hardest part of cooking is figuring out how to patch together a complete meal. So I added a little shout-out to the end of each main recipe with one menu idea (see *Great with: . . .*)—usually the simplest and most delicious one I would definitely serve myself. Mix, match, and go wild, but these can be your starting points if you need a little inspiration.

how to get the most out of the recipes

The recipes in this book work with or without a decoder, but just in case you're wondering what that little eyeball is about, or what it means when coconut water is "divided," here's a guide—to the practices used in most modern recipes, and the ways I tried to make this book extra-helpful.

STANDARD PRACTICES FOR MOST MODERN RECIPES

divided: A little *psst* that the ingredient is used in more than one place (so you don't toss it all in at once).

salt: You can use whatever salt you have, even though this book mostly calls for fine sea salt. Just round up with coarser ones—e.g., double the amount if you're using Diamond Crystal kosher salt. Most importantly, salt to taste (see right).

ingredient list prep: Most recipes assume you'll do any chopping, peeling, and crushing before you start cooking. If you want to sneak ahead and get a pot boiling or the oven heating, that's smart, too!

to taste: Literally taste, add a little, taste again. (Repeat.)

crushed peppercorns vs. peppercorns, crushed: That comma actually matters. In the first, you crush before measuring—and you'll end up with more in the teaspoon than in the second (which is measured whole first, then crushed).

make ahead and store: You don't have to do either one, but if you want to, here's how.

THE RECIPES IN THIS BOOK

INTRO
Where I tell you about how this recipe will change your life, and the genius behind it.

bold instructions
The key part of each step, so you can get the gist of how a recipe comes together and keep track of where you are (plus, tips on any longer cook or chill times).

orange tools
A quickly scannable list of the equipment you'll need (and backups). Peek at the ingredient list, too—it might call for a little chopping or peeling.

Great with
Just one idea for an easy meal (of zillions).

👁 p. 000
A heads-up there's more helpful intel elsewhere in the book, like a visual guide (Is My Chicken Done? page 170) or step-by-step illustration (How to Handle Hot Chiles Without Spicy Surprises, page 70).

WHEN WRITER YI JUN LOH'S sister went vegetarian, the long-simmered chicken and pork-based soups that fed their family in Malaysia needed to be rethought. Jun's mom reached for coconut water, which, thanks to its popularity as a healthful, hydrating drink, is easy to find at grocery stores—even gas stations—all over. And unlike packaged boxes of stock, it's made up of just one ingredient that happens to be vegan: the water that comes out of young coconuts, a shockingly good substitute for the umami and subtle sweetness of meaty bone broths.

You can use this trick to quickly give a backbone to any soup or stew, but a good place to start is Jun's riff on his mom's ABC soup, a simple, comforting Malaysian chicken soup, which has not one but two doses of coconut water. The first is subtly steeped with the vegetables; the second remains light and fresh.

one-pot coconut water abc soup

from yi jun loh

SERVES 4 TO 6

4 cups (950ml) water

8 cups (1.9L) coconut water, divided

1 teaspoon fine sea salt

3 medium white or yellow onions, peeled and quartered 🥬 p. 256

4 medium potatoes, peeled and cut into 1½-inch (4cm) chunks (I especially like starchy russets here)

2 medium carrots, peeled and cut into 1-inch (2.5cm) chunks

2 medium tomatoes, quartered (well-drained canned tomatoes are fine)

1 teaspoon crushed white peppercorns, or to taste 🥬 p. 59

1   **about 1 hour before you want soup, simmer the broth**: In a deep pot, combine the water, 4 cups (950ml) of the coconut water, and salt. Bring this to a boil, then turn it down to a simmer.

2   **simmer the vegetables**: Using a colander, strainer, or slotted spoon (to prevent splashing), carefully lower the onions and potatoes into the pot and simmer on very low heat, uncovered, for 30 minutes. Then, add the carrots and tomatoes in the same way and simmer for 20 to 30 minutes more. The vegetables should all be close to falling apart at this point, which is perfect.

3   **season and eat**: Stir in the crushed peppercorns and the remaining 4 cups (950ml) coconut water and bring to a final boil. Season to taste with salt, and serve hot.

make ahead and store: The soup will keep well in a sealed container in the refrigerator for 1 week. Reheat in the microwave or in a pot over medium-high heat on the stovetop until steaming hot.

Great with: Honey-sautéed spinach (page 208) and a cup of tea.

speedy, sensible workday breakfasts

SOME CHEFS INSIST that you have to scramble eggs low and slow—as in, 15 minutes of slow, patient stirring—unless you like eggs as dry as a loofah. They are wrong, and we can all get on with our mornings.

Mandy Lee, author of *The Art of Escapism Cooking*, has sped up the beautifully soft, custardy scrambled egg to just *15 seconds*. Usually, cooking eggs this fast and hot would make their delicate protein network seize up and squeeze out moisture if you cooked them just a few moments too long. But Mandy adds a little starch, which gets in the way of those protein connections, keeping even (*oops!*) slightly overcooked eggs tender and buttery. Her ratios are perfect but flexible—with a little practice, you can eyeball it all.

Even if you skimp on the butter, the starch will have dramatic effects. I do recommend going all in, though. You won't even need to butter your toast.

magic 15-second creamy scrambled eggs
from mandy lee

SERVES 1, BUT DOUBLES WELL

1 tablespoon plus 1½ teaspoons whole milk*

2¼ teaspoons potato starch, tapioca starch, or cornstarch*

3 large eggs

Salt

3 tablespoons unsalted butter*

1 **whisk the starch & eggs:** In a medium bowl, whisk together the milk and starch until it's smooth and lump-free. Crack in your eggs, add a pinch or two of salt (I like about ⅛ teaspoon fine sea salt for every 2 eggs, and you'll quickly figure out what you like), and whisk until smooth. Set a plate by the stove—these eggs move fast.

2 **heat your pan:** Heat a medium nonstick skillet over medium-high heat, until it feels quite warm when you hover your palm over the pan. To check if it's ready, flick a drop of water in with your fingers—it should sizzle.

3 **start cooking (on the heat):** Add the butter to the hot skillet. When the butter is melted and bubbly, but before it browns, scrape in the eggs with a silicone spatula. Without stirring, wait for the edges of the eggs to start to bubble up, about 3 seconds.

4 **scramble (off the heat):** Now, slide the skillet off the heat to a cool burner and start scraping the spatula around the bottom and sides of the pan, making one full circle per second for about 12 seconds, until the eggs have absorbed the butter but still look a little wetter and looser than you want them to be. (If you use a smaller skillet or more eggs, it will need more time—feel free to move it back to the heat if needed.)

5 **eat:** Slide the eggs onto the plate now—they'll finish cooking in the residual heat. (If you wait until they look just right, they'll get firmer and drier on the plate but still taste pretty good thanks to the starch buffer.) Eat right away.

Great with: A sprinkle of chives and black pepper, a toasted English muffin, and a cup of strong tea.

*Scaling & Swapping
To scale up or down, this works out to 1½ teaspoons milk, ¾ teaspoon starch, and 1 tablespoon butter per egg. For the creamiest eggs, Mandy prefers potato or tapioca starch, which gel at a lower temperature. But if cornstarch is all you can find, it will still be delicious.

A starchy slurry blocks egg proteins from linking and tightening

Even off the heat, the eggs cook in the still-very-hot pan

3 MORE WAYS TO SCRAMBLE

Start with whisking the starch and eggs in step 1 on page 10, then . . .

Tamagoyaki-inspired soft scramble like *New York Times* cooking writer Eric Kim:

- Whisk in a grated garlic clove, ½ teaspoon soy sauce, and 1 teaspoon sugar in step 1.

- Cook the eggs in 1 teaspoon toasted sesame oil, no butter.

- Top with crushed or snipped roasted seaweed snack, and serve with rice alongside.

Fatoot samneh (toasted pita and scrambled eggs), a Yemenite-Jewish dish, like *The Jewish Cookbook* author Leah Koenig:

- Rip up a stale pita bread.

- Sizzle and brown the pita in the buttery skillet, stirring often, then scramble in the eggs.

- Drizzle with mild honey or the Yemenite hot sauce s'chug.

Scrambled eggs with dried mint like *Bottom of the Pot* author Naz Deravian:

- Add a scant ½ teaspoon dried mint in step 1.

- Optionally, just before your eggs are done, stir in a tablespoon of plain yogurt.

- Serve with your favorite bread and black tea.

THE FIRST JOY of this recipe is frying your eggs in what feels like a little too much bubbling olive oil, spooning it over the egg as you go. This way, you get crispy edges and luscious middles without having to risk a flip and, best of all, *control* over exactly which parts of the egg you want to cook more, simply by aiming your spoon.

The second joy is in the tinkering. Here, Christopher Hirsheimer and Melissa Hamilton of the Canal House cookbooks toss in a little pimentón (smoked paprika). In seconds, the heat of the oil toasts the ground spice, deepening and unleashing its flavor. But you could just as easily perk up the oil with other spices like red pepper flakes or cumin seeds, fresh herb sprigs like sage or rosemary, or sliced alliums like garlic or scallions. You don't have to worry much about any of them burning in the sizzling oil, because before you know it, the egg is done, and so is your breakfast. If you'd like to brighten the oil before swiping your toast through, stir in a little vinegar or lemon juice at the end, just like salad dressing.

pimentón fried eggs

from christopher hirsheimer & melissa hamilton

**SERVES 2, BUT
SCALES WELL***

¼ cup (60ml) olive oil

½ teaspoon pimentón
(smoked paprika)

4 large eggs

Salt

Crusty bread, for serving

1 **make the spiced oil:** Grab two small bowls and set them by the stove. Heat the olive oil in a heavy medium skillet over medium-high heat until quite warm. If you sprinkle in a teeny pinch of the pimentón, it should sizzle. Add the pimentón and gently tip the skillet to swirl it around so it dissolves into the oil.

2 **fry your eggs:** Crack open 2 eggs into the small bowls, then gently pour them into the skillet, reducing the heat if the oil's spattering a lot. Fry the eggs, carefully spooning the hot olive oil over the eggs, tipping the pan carefully if needed to collect enough olive oil to spoon up, until the whites are firm and the yolks are soft. You can feel how done they are by gently poking the egg yolk and white with the back of your spoon. With a wide spatula, lift the fried eggs onto a plate, then repeat with the remaining 2 eggs.

3 **eat:** Season with salt to taste. Serve the eggs with the oil spooned on top and bread to swipe it all up.

Great with: Sliced, salted tomatoes to dunk in the smoky oil.

*For More Eggs (or Fewer)
You can scale this recipe up or down, but even if you want to fry just one egg, you still want enough oil in the pan to spoon over easily.

A snug pan means you need less oil to form a puddle

Smoked paprika is just the beginning!

red pepper flakes

sumac

scallions

turmeric

common fried egg woes
(& how to fix them)

Egg snafus happen, whether you're using the olive oil–frying technique on page 14 or any other. But there are solutions to them all—and sometimes, what feels like a failure might lead you to your new favorite breakfast.

it stuck!

THIS TIME

Quickly scramble it up, somewhat like Spanish revueltos, in which eggs often start whole and end scrambled. Or hide it in a sandwich. Everything tastes good there.

NEXT TIME

Get the pan a little hotter and add more fat, or just use a nonstick pan.

my yolk is hard.

THIS TIME

Mash it onto toast with extra butter.

NEXT TIME

Pull it off the heat sooner, and be sure to press the white and yolk gently with your spoon or spatula to check how they're coming along.

my whites are runny.

THIS TIME

How runny are we talking? Translucent: Throw the egg back in the pan. Opaque and mostly firm: Close your eyes and go for it, like people do with sunny-side-up eggs every day.

NEXT TIME

Make sure you prod the thickest part closest to the yolk to see that it's firm.

my spatula got stuck to the egg and it's a big mess.

THIS TIME

It's still a tasty mess.

NEXT TIME

Have patience and wait for the white to firm up before you start fiddling.

my yolk broke!

THIS TIME

To keep some runny yolk intact, avoid flipping and either cover the pan or spoon some extra oil or butter over any undercooked whites. Or just negotiate with other eaters—maybe someone likes it that way!

NEXT TIME

It happens! Try cracking your egg into a small bowl before sliding it gently into the pan.

MAKING A QUICK batch of oatmeal each day can be a happy, steadying ritual. Finding the sticky pot still soaking in the sink at 6 p.m. is not. So food stylist and *The Joys of Baking* author Samantha Seneviratne switched to a nonstick skillet—a trick she picked up in a test kitchen at some point in her career, but really put to use when feeding her toddler, Arthur. Not only is the skillet much easier to clean, but the oats also cook down swifter and creamier, as they bubble down over a wider surface area.

The following basic ratio works with any milk, mix-ins, and toppings (see more of Samantha's ideas on page 20), but you'll want this chocolate-almond combo for mornings in need of glee. It will smell like hot cocoa as you stir it and remind you of the chocolatey cereals little-kid-you weren't supposed to have—with a nutty, bittersweet depth to hug your grown-up heart.

cocoa almond oatmeal
from samantha seneviratne

SERVES 1*

½ cup (50g) old-fashioned rolled oats

1¼ cups (300ml) unsweetened almond milk, plus more for serving

Salt

4 teaspoons cocoa powder

2 tablespoons creamy or chunky almond butter

Maple syrup (optional)

1 **simmer the oats:** To a medium nonstick skillet, add the oats, almond milk, a pinch of salt, and the cocoa. Bring to a simmer over medium heat, stirring frequently and scraping the bottom and sides with a silicone spatula, until the oats are tender and creamy, about 5 minutes. Reduce the heat if it starts boiling too wildly, and don't wander away or it might boil over on you. Stop cooking when the oatmeal is a little looser than you want, as it will thicken as it cools.

2 **top and eat:** Swirl in the almond butter and maple syrup. Add more milk if you'd like. Serve hot and clean up fast.

store: Leftover oatmeal will keep well in a container in the fridge for a few days, though it will thicken as it cools. Reheat in the microwave or in a nonstick skillet over medium heat, stirring in a splash of milk or water.

Great with: Coffee. Maybe a peach or pear on the side.

*More Oatmeal!
This recipe scales up well, but it might take a few extra minutes to cook. At any scale, make sure your pan isn't more than two-thirds full since it will bubble up as it simmers. An 8-inch (20cm) skillet is great for one serving; go with 10-inch (25cm) or larger for a double batch.

Skip the cocoa and almond butter on page 18 and ...

banana-cacao nib:

- Swap in ¾ cup (175ml) coconut milk and ½ cup (120ml) whole milk and add a big pinch of ground cinnamon to the pan.

- Top with cacao nibs and sliced bananas at the end. (It will taste like Chunky Monkey ice cream.)

raspberry-cardamom:

- Go with whole milk.

- After cooking, swirl in 2 teaspoons raspberry jam and a pinch of ground cardamom.

- Scatter fresh raspberries on top.

nutty multigrain:

- Stick with whole milk.

- Stir in ¼ cup (50g) leftover cooked grains like quinoa or farro p. 87 toward the end.

- Sprinkle with chopped pecans and blueberries.

top with anything fresh or crunchy the morning of

smash the berries and soak the oats the night before

how to make oatmeal while you sleep

Filling a couple jars with overnight oats (or its grandparent, Bircher muesli, popularized by the Swiss physician Maximilian Bircher-Benner in the early 1900s) is one of the easier ways to wake up feeling ready for life. But a surprising number of recipes still ask us to grate an apple or layer in chia puddings or make other interventions the morning of.

This template from Anna Jones's cookbook *The Modern Cook's Year* is far simpler, mostly smashing and pouring. In her precise recipe, Anna uses raspberries, hazelnuts, hazelnut milk, orange juice, and coconut yogurt, but feel free to take her basic ratio below and run (or, more accurately, sleep). You can even toast and chop the nuts ahead of time (or buy them roasted), allowing all sharp tools to be optional before 8 a.m.

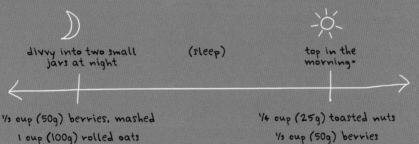

divvy into two small jars at night

(sleep)

top in the morning*

⅓ cup (50g) berries, mashed
1 cup (100g) rolled oats
3 tablespoons juice
1 cup (250ml) milk

¼ cup (25g) toasted nuts
⅓ cup (50g) berries
¼ cup (60ml) yogurt

*save half for topping jar 2 tomorrow, or share with a friend!

THE REWARD-TO-EFFORT RATIO of making your own granola is ever in your favor: All you have to do is stir and bake, and you'll start to resent boxed granola's one-note sweetness and muted crunch. Homemade granola is crackly, fresh, and exactly the way you like it.

But even among other simple, rewarding granola recipes, this one from Jenné Claiborne, author of the book and blog *Sweet Potato Soul*, stands out. It calls for less stirring, shorter baking, and fewer ingredients than most—you won't even need oil, since the fat from ground sesame seeds in the Middle Eastern cooking staple tahini adds all the crisping power you need. I start thinking about it the second I wake up.

tahini pistachio granola
from jenné claiborne

SERVES 4

½ cup (125g) well-stirred tahini

⅓ cup (80ml) maple syrup

1 teaspoon vanilla extract

¼ teaspoon fine sea salt

2 cups (180g) old-fashioned rolled oats

½ to 1 cup (60 to 120g) shelled raw pistachios (or another nut or pepitas)

2 tablespoons chia seeds

1 **stir everything together:** Heat the oven to 350°F (175°C) with a rack in the center. Line a sheet pan with a silicone baking mat or parchment paper. In a large mixing bowl, stir together the tahini, maple syrup, vanilla, and salt with a silicone spatula until it's smooth and evenly combined. Stir in the oats, pistachios, and chia seeds.

2 **bake the granola:** Spread the wet, sticky oats onto the sheet pan in a thin, even layer. Bake for 10 minutes, then, using oven mitts, take the pan out of the oven and stir the granola—this will help it finish baking evenly. Return the pan to the oven and bake until the granola is dry and golden brown, another 5 to 10 minutes. Keep a close eye toward the end to make sure it doesn't start to burn at the edges.

3 **eat:** Let the granola cool completely to crisp up, about 20 minutes, before breaking it into clumps with your hands. Eat with your favorite yogurt or milk, in a smoothie bowl or parfait (a handy on-the-go breakfast in a jar), or by the handful as a snack.

store: The granola keeps well in a sealed container at room temperature for at least a week, or as long as it lasts.

Great with: Blueberries, plain yogurt, a little olive oil, and a pinch of salt.

3 MORE WAYS TO RIFF LIKE JENNÉ

play with spices—Jenné likes ½ teaspoon ground cinnamon, and I will put a few gratings of whole nutmeg (from a Microplane) on just about anything.

stir in ½ cup (80g) peeled, grated sweet potato (shredded on the small holes of a box grater) before baking for earthy sweetness (and a breakfast vegetable!).

sprinkle in dried rose petals or other edible dried flowers after baking when you're feeling fancy.

Stir a few ingredients, bake 15 minutes, granola all week!

Have patience—it'll crisp up as it cools

CREAMY TAHINI MILK
from gena hamshaw

Making your own nut or seed milk isn't tricky, but it does require an overnight soak, a muscular blender, and a straining step I don't always have patience for. On her blog, *The Full Helping*, Gena Hamshaw shared a simpler milk based on tahini, the creamy Middle Eastern sesame seed paste. For times you'd like a less smoky flavor, you can riff on this idea with any nut butter.

MAKES ABOUT 3½ CUPS (830ML)

3 or 4 pitted dates (or more for sweeter milk, or a splash of maple syrup in a hurry)

Warm water, for soaking

½ cup (125g) well-stirred tahini (roasted or raw)

3 cups (710ml) filtered water

Pinch of salt

1 Soak the dates in warm water in a bowl for about 30 minutes. Drain. Blend the drained dates, tahini, filtered water, and salt with an immersion blender (or regular blender) till very smooth.

2 Store in a sealed jar in the refrigerator for up to 4 days. Shake before using if the tahini has settled to the bottom.

3 Use in your coffee, smoothies 🥄 p. 26, and definitely oatmeal 🥄 p. 18.

WHEN ANITA SHEPHERD, vegan chef and founder of Anita's Yogurt, cut back on sugars in her smoothies to evade migraines, she started experimenting with frozen vegetables like cucumber, cauliflower, and beets, inspired by the versions her coconut yogurt fans were posting online. (This one is a riff on the Walk the Plank smoothie Anita used to make on holistic nutrition coach Deborah Smith's Green Pirate Juice truck, with just about everything green on the truck.) The key to Anita's smoothies: a full teaspoon of vanilla extract. "The vanilla gives you that smoothie feel without added sweetness," she told me. "Omit it, and things veer more toward liquid salad."

On the next few pages are four of Anita's favorites, but she encourages playing around with her no-longer-secret formula: 1 cup frozen vegetable + 1 cup frozen fleshy fruit (berries or something else not-too-sweet) + ½ cup orange or pineapple juice + ⅓ cup yogurt + 1 teaspoon vanilla extract + any optional flavorful herbs, greens, or powders you like.

not-too-sweet pineapple green smoothie

from anita shepherd

SERVES 1

1 seedless English cucumber*

1 cup (140g) frozen pineapple chunks

1 cup (30g) baby spinach

Handful of flat-leaf parsley

Handful of basil leaves

½ cup (120ml) orange juice

⅓ cup (80ml) plain Greek yogurt (nondairy or dairy)

1 tablespoon spirulina (optional)

1 teaspoon vanilla extract

1   **the night before (or earlier), chop and freeze your cucumber**: On a cutting board, peel the cucumber with a vegetable peeler (optional). With a chef's knife, chop into ½-inch (1.3cm) pieces. Add to a zippered freezer bag in a single layer and press out excess air. Try not to let the pieces mash together too much—big frozen chunks will be tough on the blender. Freeze flat in a single layer until solid, at least 3 hours.

2   **blend and eat**: With a blender or immersion blender, blend 1 cup (130g) of frozen cucumber with all other ingredients until thick, smooth, and creamy. If your blender is struggling, keep scraping everything down with a silicone spatula and leave it to soften for a few minutes or add a splash more liquid before blending again. Taste and add more of anything, if you like. Serve immediately in a tall glass.

Great with: Tahini granola (page 22) and a big spoonful of extra yogurt on top.

*Breakfasts for Days

Unless you want to snack on it instead, go ahead and freeze all of the chopped cucumber at once. Future smoothies will be that much faster, and it's easy to break off just what you need (more smoothie library inspiration on page 28).

Chop any veg and fruit that isn't bite-size
(or buy them pre-chopped and frozen)

The safest way
to pit avocados?
Put your index
and middle finger
on either side
of the pit, then
push the skin
directly behind
the pit with your
thumb (thanks
to TikTok user
@_mynameischo)

Freeze in a smoothie library to mix and match all week

3 MORE WAYS TO RIFF LIKE ANITA

Start with ½ cup (120ml) orange juice, ⅓ cup (80ml) plain Greek yogurt, and 1 teaspoon vanilla extract like on page 26, and then add . . .

matcha mint:

- ½ cup (65g) frozen cucumber
- ½ cup (75g) frozen avocado
- 1 to 1½ cups (155 to 235g) frozen honeydew (depending on how sweet it is)
- 1 big handful fresh mint or tarragon leaves (or half of each)
- 2 teaspoons matcha powder

red velvet, inspired by functional nutrition coach Isa de Burgh:

- 1 cup (165g) frozen cooked beets (feel free to buy pre-cooked in the produce section)
- 1 cup (135g) frozen raspberries
- 2 tablespoons + 1 teaspoon cocoa powder

açaí:

- 1 cup (110g) frozen cauliflower
- ¾ cup (115g) frozen blueberries and/or cherries
- 1 (3.5-ounce/100g) packet frozen açaí (for easier blending, chop the açaí into a few pieces and let it soften a little)
- For a riff on Brazilian açaí bowls, top with chopped fresh fruit and roasted, unsalted peanuts.

2 genius toasts

The avocado toast that shocked and delighted the internet (no, you really won't need salt). And a brilliant trick for faster, arguably better, egg salad, without peeling any eggs.

MAKES 2 TARTINES

2 (1-inch/2.5cm-thick) slices sourdough bread

1 ripe medium avocado

1 medium banana

1 teaspoon finely grated lime zest 👁 p. 203

2 tablespoons freshly squeezed lime juice 👁 p. 203

Red pepper flakes

1 to 2 tablespoons honey

AVOCADO TARTINES WITH BANANA & LIME
from apollonia poilâne

1 Set the sourdough on a sheet pan and, using your oven's broiler, toast it on just one side until golden—the bread should be about 4 inches (10cm) away from the heat.

2 On a cutting board with a paring knife, pit and peel the avocado 👁 p. 28 and coarsely mash it onto the toasted side of the bread with a fork. Slice and arrange the banana on top.

3 Sprinkle with the lime zest and juice and a pinch of red pepper flakes. Drizzle with the honey to taste and eat.

**SERVES 2 (OR 1 PLUS
A SANDWICH TOMORROW)**

6 large eggs

1 tablespoon unsalted butter

¼ cup (30g) thinly sliced
yellow onion 👁 p. 256

¼ cup (35g) chopped ham

¼ cup (55g) mayonnaise

2 tablespoons finely chopped
celery (optional)

Salt and freshly ground black pepper

Toast, for serving

Celery leaves (optional), for topping

FRIED EGG SALAD

from aki kamozawa & h. alexander talbot

1   Crack your eggs into a medium bowl. Heat a 10-inch (25cm) nonstick pan over
medium heat, with a lid or sheet pan nearby. Melt the butter, add the onion and
ham, and cook, stirring with a wooden spoon, until the onion is soft.

2   Turn the heat to medium-low, gently pour the eggs around the pan, and cover.
With oven mitts, lift the lid to check on the eggs after a couple of minutes, and
remove from the heat when the whites are firm and the yolks are as runny as
you like when gently poked with the spoon.

3   Slide the eggs into another medium bowl and chop with kitchen scissors. Stir in
the mayo and celery, plus salt and pepper to taste. Serve warm on toast topped
with salt, pepper, and celery leaves. Leftovers are delicious cold the next day.

weekend fun breakfasts

MANY WILL TELL you the fluffiest pancakes come from separating eggs, whipping the whites into a foamy cloud, and folding them gently into the batter. But a) this is a lot to take on at 8 a.m. and b) the batter often starts tall and proud but, by the end of a big batch, deflates like a melted milkshake.

Great news: You needn't whip the eggs at all—at least in this recipe. (And you can make the batter entirely the night before.) Made famous on *The Kitchn* by longtime contributor Dana Velden, this recipe requires only *stirring* in the egg whites at the end. The cakes are just as fluffy as if you'd whipped them (I checked).

Rose Levy Beranbaum, author of *The Baking Bible*, explained to me that the last-minute unwhipped egg white provides support that's especially stable, a technique sometimes used to keep soufflés from collapsing: "Whipping egg whites to soft or stiff peaks adds more air but also, as the egg white cells enlarge, the membrane gets thinner and thinner and is more fragile," eventually popping and huffing out much of the air. But not here: You just get glorious fluff, from beginning of batch to end.

lofty buttermilk pancakes
from dana velden

SERVES 4 TO 6

2½ cups (315g) all-purpose flour*

2 tablespoons sugar

¾ teaspoon fine sea salt

1 teaspoon baking powder

1 teaspoon baking soda

2 large eggs, separated
p. 37

2 cups (475ml) buttermilk**

½ cup (120ml) whole milk

10 tablespoons (140g) unsalted butter, melted and cooled p. 204

1 tablespoon neutral oil, such as canola

1 **set up your station**: The best way to eat pancakes is fresh off the stove. But if you don't want to flip pancakes through breakfast, heat the oven to 225°F (105°C) to keep them warm as they come off the skillet. Set an ovenproof cooling rack inside a large sheet pan and stick them in the center of the oven. If you don't have a cooling rack, you can hack one by laying out Mason jar lid rings or metal cookie cutters, or even lay the pancakes directly on the oven racks—you want your pancakes to be in a single layer, with warm air circulating around them to keep them crisp, not soggy.

2 **mix dry, mix wet**: In a large bowl, whisk together the flour, sugar, salt, baking powder, and baking soda. In a medium bowl, whisk the egg yolks, buttermilk, and milk. Add the melted, cooled butter and whisk until well combined.

3 **make your batter**: With a silicone spatula, scrape the wet ingredients into the dry ingredients and stir until barely combined—lumps are okay. Add the egg whites and stir just until no visible streaks of egg white remain, then set the batter aside for 5 minutes while you heat your pan.

4 **start frying**: Heat a large cast-iron or nonstick skillet over medium heat. When hot, pour in ½ teaspoon of the neutral oil and swirl to coat the pan. When the oil shimmers but isn't yet smoking, about 30 seconds, lower the heat to medium-low and use a large soup spoon or ¼-cup (60ml) measure to drop in heaping scoops of pancake batter a good 2 inches (5cm) away from each other and the sides of the pan p. 36.

continued

***go whole grain**
Swap in whole-wheat flour for the all-purpose flour and make the batter the night before to let the grainier flour soften, like sourdough pro Josey Baker does.

****No Buttermilk?**
Thin yogurt with a little milk—about 1⅓ cups (315ml) plain yogurt with ⅔ cup (160ml) milk here.

lofty buttermilk pancakes
continued

5 **flip your pancakes**: Cook until the bubbles that form on the edges of the pancakes look dry and airy, about 2½ minutes. (If the pancake burns or the oil starts smoking, lower the heat.) Slide a wide spatula (preferably not metal if you're using a nonstick skillet) gently under one side of the pancake and lift to peek underneath. If the pancake is golden brown, flip and cook on the other side until the bottom of the pancake is golden brown, another 2 to 2½ minutes.

6 **eat**: With the spatula, lift each pancake from the skillet onto a plate to serve immediately, or onto the cooling rack in the oven (in a single layer) to keep warm. Wipe any stray crumbs or burnt oil out of the skillet with a clean kitchen towel or paper towel, add a little more oil, and continue to cook the remaining batter, adjusting the heat as needed. Serve hot.

make ahead and store: The batter can be made the night before and stored in an airtight container in the fridge with no loss in fluffiness. Leftover pancakes keep well in a container in the fridge for up to a week (or in the freezer for a month or so) and warm up well in a toaster or on a sheet pan under a broiler, flipping to toast each side.

Great with: Soft butter and maple syrup or berries and sour cream.

Popped bubbles + golden underneath = ready to flip

Sprinkle on berries, or sliced fruit, chopped nuts, coconut, and so on.

how minimalists separate eggs

The standard way to separate eggs (without a special gizmo) is to pass the yolk back and forth between the cracked eggshell halves, letting the white ooze into a bowl below.

But using just your hands is faster and less likely to puncture the yolk—and works even when your shell doesn't split into two tidy halves. It will feel a little deviant and messy, which is almost the best part (and your hands weren't staying clean anyway).

1) grab three bowls

2) Crack an egg with conviction on a flat counter or cutting board

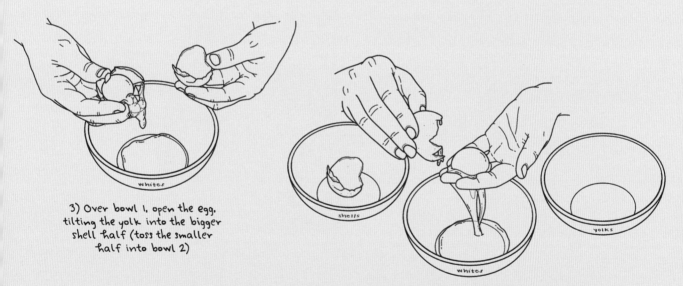

3) Over bowl 1, open the egg, tilting the yolk into the bigger shell half (toss the smaller half into bowl 2)

4) Gently tip the yolk into your other hand, letting the white fall through your fingers

5) Plop the yolk into bowl 3, and repeat!

6) Wash your hands and your surface with hot, soapy water; no one will know you've been playing with raw egg

what your pancake flipper's station should look like

Saturday morning pancakes are as much about the ritual as the sticky, buttery results.

Here's how to set up your pancake routine to be stress-free and repeatable, whether you're using Dana Velden's Lofty Buttermilk Pancakes recipe (page 34) or any other.

If your kitchen allows it, consider skipping the warming oven and slinging all the pancakes straight onto eaters' plates. (And assume it will turn into a dance party.)

side plate for cook's snacks (important)

heading to a warming oven (optional)

neutral oil for re-upping the pa[n]

long-handled scooper

your biggest skillets (two at once means faster pancakes)

A Few Good Pancake-Flipping Songs

"He's Misstra Know-It-All" by Stevie Wonder	"Cool Cat" by Queen
"Grey Seal" by Elton John	"Jealous Guy-Live" by Donny Hathaway
"Under Attack" by ABBA	"Lost in the Supermarket" by The Clash

common pancake woes
(& how to fix them)

Pancakes can be a little finicky at the start, and the first one is always a wild card. But they also offer the rare opportunity to course-correct with every flip, and soon you (and your burners) will know exactly what you're doing.

Here are some simple solutions to all kinds of bugaboos. Also: Consider making a double batch, so you can eat all your test cakes along the way.

why won't they stop burning?

THIS TIME

Lean into the bitter notes and add punchy toppings that won't be overpowered. Clementines, crème fraîche, honey? Salted butter and fig jam? Yes, those should do it.

NEXT TIME

Let your pan preheat at a lower temperature and longer, and keep adjusting the heat as you go.

they're raw inside—eek.

THIS TIME

Throw them back in the pan or microwave.

NEXT TIME

Lower your heat and wait till those bubbles have popped before flipping. If the pancakes are weirdly thick and not cooking through, thin the batter with a splash of milk.

they're unevenly browned.

THIS TIME

Bring on the toppings!

NEXT TIME

Use your biggest burner(s) and heaviest skillets, and preheat them longer to even out the heat. Rotate the pancakes as needed.

there were three spoonfuls, but now they're all one big pancake.

THIS TIME

One big pancake!? Flip it carefully and it will be the one everyone fights over.

NEXT TIME

Try smaller scoops of batter, more spaced apart.

they're soggy.

THIS TIME

A quick toast or flash under the broiler (don't walk away!) should crisp them up.

NEXT TIME

Don't stack them. And consider eating them hot and fresh out of the pan.

they fell apart when i flipped them.

THIS TIME

More for the cook and trusted associates.

NEXT TIME

Wait till they look firm and a little dry, not gooey, before flipping, and turn down the heat if needed. (Hint: If your pancake flops off the edge of your spatula, give it a little more time.)

THE FREEING GENRE of make-ahead breakfast casseroles lets you knock out all the thinking and doing the day before, unlike trying to flip fried eggs for a crowd of hungry people (not recommended). But in all of their ingenious practicality, breakfast casseroles can often feel utilitarian at best.

But what if instead of a casserole that you cut in tidy rectangles, it was borderline dessert? Namely, a bread pudding, like this one pastry-chef-turned-food-writer Shilpa Uskokovic makes out of custard-puffed croissants? It's still a mix-at-night, bake-in-the-morning operation, gloriously rich but not ultra-sweet. As Shilpa told me, extra berries and yogurt on top would "push the boat further into breakfast-y waters."

glorious croissant bread pudding
from shilpa uskokovic

SERVES 6 TO 8

4 to 5 large plain croissants
(about 250g)

2 cups (475ml) heavy cream

1½ cups (355ml) whole milk

1 cup (200g) sugar

3 large eggs

2 large egg yolks ☞ p. 37

1 teaspoon fine sea salt

2 teaspoons vanilla paste
or extract

1 cup (170g) dark chocolate
chips

1 cup (120g) raspberries,
fresh or frozen

½ cup (45g) sliced almonds

Fresh raspberries and
Greek yogurt, for serving
(optional)

1   **the night before you want bread pudding, get started:** With a serrated knife on a large cutting board, slice the croissants into 1½-inch (4cm) cubes (about the size of a walnut in the shell).

2   **make the custard:** Heat the cream, milk, and sugar in a medium saucepan over medium-low heat, stirring occasionally with a silicone spatula, until the sugar dissolves and the liquid just starts to simmer gently. Turn off the heat.

3   In a large, heavy bowl (or a not-so-heavy bowl nestled into a damp kitchen towel to steady it), whisk together the eggs, yolks, salt, and vanilla. Slowly pour or ladle the hot cream mixture over the eggs while whisking fiercely to combine. Toss in the cubed croissants and stir with the spatula until all of the croissant pieces are evenly coated and mostly submerged. Cover and refrigerate for up to 24 hours. (Feel free to measure out the chocolate chips, raspberries, and almonds and store them covered for easy mixing in the morning, too—the raspberries should go back in the fridge or freezer.)

4   **about 2 hours before you want bread pudding, get ready to bake:** Heat the oven to 325°F (165°C) with an oven rack positioned in the center.

5   Just before baking, stir the chocolate chips and raspberries (if using frozen, no need to thaw) into the croissant-y custard. Pour into a 9-inch (23cm) square pan or other baking dish with a 2-quart (1.9L) capacity. Scatter the sliced almonds on top and bake till the top of the bread pudding is lightly puffed and dry to the touch (on the croissant parts—don't touch a molten chocolate chip) and the center jiggles faintly but doesn't slosh when you shake the pan, 50 to 60 minutes.

6   **eat:** Serve warm with extra raspberries and a dollop of Greek yogurt if you like, though it's perfectly delicious plain, too.

store: Leftovers keep well, tightly covered in the refrigerator for 3 to 5 days. If you don't eat it all cold from the pan (deliriously good), try a few slices griddled ☞ p. 42.

Great with: "Fried" bacon (page 43) and strong coffee.

Start with slicing the croissants in step 1 on page 40, then . . .

salted honey-walnut:

- Add the zest of 1 large orange 👑 p. 203 and a teaspoon of ground cinnamon when heating the milky mix in step 2.

- Instead of chocolate chips, raspberries, and almonds, stir in 2½ cups (250g) toasted, chopped walnuts 👑 p. 261 in step 5.

- After baking, brush the warm bread pudding with honey and sprinkle with flaky salt.

double-chocolate:

- Bump up the cream to 2½ cups (590ml) and chocolate chips to 2 cups (340g).

- Whisk ¼ cup (20g) Dutch-processed cocoa powder into the milky mix before heating in step 2.

- Feel free to keep the raspberries and almonds (or nix one or both).

griddle it:

- Slice cold leftover pudding into slabs about 1½ inches (4cm) thick.

- Melt a teaspoon of unsalted butter in a small nonstick skillet over medium-high heat.

- Griddle slices till golden brown on one side, flip with a wide spatula, and cook until the second side is pale golden and the pudding is warmed through.

- Serve immediately with tahini and raspberry jam or salted butter and maple syrup.

JOE'S FAMOUS "FRIED" BACON
from joe's bakery

"People, it's not deep-fried," Regina Estrada, third-generation co-owner of Joe's Bakery, told Paula Forbes for *The Austin Cookbook*. But a thin layer of flour crisped on the outside makes this "fried" bacon good and crunchy enough to convince us otherwise.

Regina's grandfather Joe Avila realized the bacon for their tacos stayed crispier and kept its shape better with a coating of flour and an overnight chill. At the bakery, their family fries the bacon on a griddle, but this oven-baked method is a handy way to cook bacon evenly for a crowd at home.

SERVES AS MANY AS YOU LIKE

Thick-cut bacon
(2 to 3 strips per
bacon eater)

All-purpose flour
(about 1 tablespoon
per bacon strip)

1   **The night before you want bacon,** dip the bacon strips in a medium bowl of flour to coat completely. Shake off any loose flour and lay the strips on a parchment paper–lined sheet pan in a single layer (if you need to stack the bacon, lay parchment between each layer), cover the pan with beeswax wrap or a final layer of parchment, and refrigerate overnight.

2   In the morning, heat the oven to 400°F (200°C) and bake the bacon uncovered in a single layer (not stacked) right on the parchment-lined sheet pan(s). When the bacon is starting to brown, about 5 minutes, use tongs to flip the slices over, and continue cooking until the bacon is evenly browned and crispy, about 10 minutes total. With the tongs, move the cooked bacon to a paper towel–lined plate to drain briefly. Serve warm.

THIS IS THE rare recipe where it really doesn't matter if your brunch crew is vegan, omnivore, or anything in between. It's a staple year-round at the Los Angeles coffee shop mini-empire Go Get Em Tiger, first developed by then executive chef Ria Dolly Barbosa. After playing around with variations on socca, the crisp-edged chickpea pancake with roots in Provence and Liguria, "I was intrigued by the idea of emulating quiche in a vegan form," Ria told me. "And the soccata was born."

This version, with twists of kale and cherry tomato, was adapted by Genevieve Ko for the *Los Angeles Times*, but feel free to cycle vegetables in and out with the seasons, as Ria does. The crux is the chickpea flour, which, when hydrated with plenty of water and olive oil, behaves and tastes uncannily like beaten egg. After baking, it needs an overnight rest to set up before slicing in thick slabs and griddling like French toast, which gives you that much more time to sleep in.

chickpea soccata with tomatoes & kale
from ria dolly barbosa

SERVES 4 TO 6

Olive oil or nonstick cooking spray

¾ cup (175ml) extra-virgin olive oil, divided

6 medium or 3 large shallots, thinly sliced 🕮 p. 207

1¼ teaspoons fine sea salt, plus more to taste

1 bunch Tuscan kale, stems removed and leaves cut into 1-inch (2.5cm) pieces*
🕮 p. 48

1 pint cherry tomatoes, sliced in half

Freshly ground black pepper

1½ cups (180g) chickpea flour

1¾ cups (415ml) water

1   **the night before, get ready to bake**: Heat the oven to 350°F (175°C) with a rack in the center. Coat the inside of a 9 by 5-inch (23 by 13cm) loaf pan with olive oil or nonstick cooking spray. Line the pan with a parchment paper sling, so that the paper extends slightly up over the long sides of the pan (this will make the soccata easier to lift out 🕮 p. 47). Oil the parchment.

2   **cook the vegetables**: Heat 2 tablespoons of the olive oil in a large skillet over medium-low heat. Add the shallots and a pinch of salt and cook, stirring often with a wooden spoon, until soft and golden, 7 to 9 minutes. Turn up the heat to medium and add the kale and a pinch of salt. Cook, stirring often, until wilted, 2 to 3 minutes. Slide the pan to a cool burner (turn off the hot one), add the tomatoes, a pinch of salt, and a few grinds of pepper and stir until evenly mixed. Taste and adjust the salt and pepper to taste—it should be pleasantly salty. Scrape into the prepared loaf pan and spread evenly.

3   **make the batter**: In a large bowl, whisk the chickpea flour and 1¼ teaspoons fine sea salt. Add ½ cup (120ml) of the olive oil and whisk to combine. Add the water, ¼ cup (60ml) at a time, whisking well after each addition to smooth out the mix—it will look like pancake batter. Slowly pour the batter into the pan over the vegetables. Tap the pan on the counter to pop any air bubbles, then cover tightly with foil.

4   **bake the soccata**: Bake until set, about 1 hour—a table knife inserted in the center should come away with no liquid batter on the blade. With oven mitts, uncover the pan (save the foil) and bake until the top is golden brown in spots, another 15 to 20 minutes. Cool in the pan on a wire rack or cool stove burner until just warm, then cover tightly with the same foil and refrigerate overnight to set.

continued

*About That Kale
Tuscan kale might be labeled as lacinato kale, dinosaur kale, or cavolo nero—it's smoother and darker green than curly kale. But if curly kale is all you can find, use that!

5 **in the morning, slice, crisp, and eat**: When you're ready to eat, using the parchment sling, lift the loaf onto a cutting board and, with a chef's knife, slice off as many 1-inch-thick (2.5cm) slices as you'd like to serve. Heat the remaining 2 tablespoons olive oil in a large nonstick skillet over medium-high heat. When the oil shimmers, use a wide (not metal) spatula to add the slices, spacing them apart (you may need to do this in a couple of batches or use more than one skillet). Cook, flipping once, until browned and crisp on both sides, about 5 minutes total. Serve hot.

make ahead and store: The baked loaf can be refrigerated in a sealed container (or the covered loaf pan) for up to 3 days.

Great with: Cold brew (page 49) and a crunchy green salad (page 113).

Chickpea flour batter—a vegan secret weapon

Cook some veg (any veg really)

These parchment wings are handy for lifting out later

a few ways to dispatch a bunch of greens

The stems of sturdy greens like kale, collards, and chard take longer than the leaves to cook through, so lots of recipes ask you to discard them. But don't do that! You can always give the sliced stems a head start in the pan to soften for a few minutes before adding the leaves, or save them for stock (page 81) or Bryant Terry's Quick-Sautéed Stems (page 191).

However you plan to cook them, give them a wash, as on page 185, then pick your favorite way to navigate through the bunch:

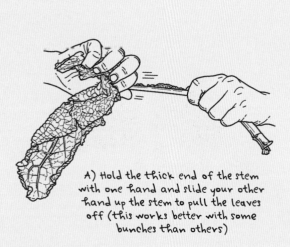

A) Hold the thick end of the stem with one hand and slide your other hand up the stem to pull the leaves off (this works better with some bunches than others)

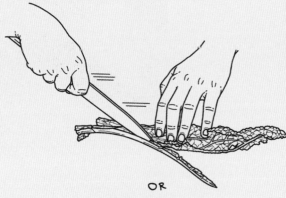

OR

B) Cut each stem out with a chef's knife on a cutting board

OR

C) Leave the stems in and embrace a little extra crunch (slicing finely will help take the edge off)

ICED CAFÉ DE OLLA
from rick martinez

Rick Martinez created this recipe for *Bon Appétit* to distill the sweet, warm spices of Mexican café de olla in iced coffee form. Make it ahead, then mix it for your brunch friends (or just for you).

SERVES 5 TO 8

¾ cup (165g) grated piloncillo or packed dark brown sugar

1 (3-inch/7.5cm) canela or cinnamon stick

5 cardamom pods, cracked

5 allspice berries

1 teaspoon black peppercorns

Pinch of salt

1 cup (240ml) water

3 wide strips orange zest, peeled on a vegetable peeler

Ice

5 to 8 cups (1.2 to 1.9L) cold-brew coffee

Unsweetened coconut milk or half-and-half, for serving

1   In a small saucepan (with a lid nearby), bring the piloncillo, canela, cardamom, allspice, peppercorns, salt, and water to a boil over high heat. Turn down the heat to low, cover, and simmer the syrup for 15 minutes. Add the orange zest and let cool. Strain the syrup through a fine-mesh strainer into a lidded jar and store in the refrigerator—it will keep well for a week.

2   For each iced café de olla, fill a glass with ice and pour in 1 cup (240ml) cold-brew coffee. Stir in 2 to 3 tablespoons syrup and top with 2 to 3 tablespoons coconut milk, to taste. (For completely smooth coconut milk, you can blend it briefly with an immersion blender first.)

HERE'S A CONUNDRUM: We're cautioned to baby our scrambled eggs, but many frittatas are left alone to parch under a broiler. Chef Andrew Feinberg has a more loving way. "Instead of cooking the eggs quickly in a hot oven," he told me, "I cook them slowly in a low oven, and the result is a very custardy and creamy texture that traditional frittatas do not have." And slow is relative—the eggs cook through in about 20 minutes while you do the dishes.

This particular recipe is a wonder: Searing the broccoli in olive oil before roasting leaves it with a deeply browned, crunchy crust like a steak. And topping with lemon juice, Parmesan, and fruity olive oil will change how you season your eggs. Make it ahead for brunch and spend your morning sipping tea instead.

But, even more usefully, Andrew's basic slow-baking technique in step 5 can work for any frittata and become your every-week meal-planning ritual (without needing to meal-plan—see page 54 for more ideas).

slow-baked broccoli frittata
from andrew feinberg

SERVES 4

10 large eggs

2½ tablespoons finely grated Parmigiano Reggiano, plus more for serving

Fine sea salt

40 turns from a black pepper mill

1 (1-pound/450g) head of broccoli (4 cups/360g once trimmed)

6 to 7 tablespoons (90 to 105ml) extra-virgin olive oil, divided

½ red onion, thinly sliced ☞ p. 256

1 heaping tablespoon chopped garlic ☞ p. 257

¼ teaspoon red pepper flakes

Lemon wedges, for serving

1 **mix up the eggs:** Heat the oven to 400°F (200°C) with a rack in the center. Into a large bowl, crack the eggs and whisk together with the Parmigiano Reggiano, ½ teaspoon salt, and black pepper and set aside.

2 **sear the broccoli:** On a cutting board with a chef's knife, cut the broccoli into florets about 2 inches (5cm) long and peel and slice the stems ☞ p. 53, making sure to cut big florets in halves or quarters so all are evenly sized and have a good, flat surface for searing. In a 10- to 11-inch (25 to 28cm) ovenproof nonstick skillet, heat 4 tablespoons (60ml) of the olive oil over medium-high heat, then add the broccoli in a single layer. Let the broccoli get nicely browned on one side, about 5 minutes, then turn it all over with a wide, nonmetal spatula and season with a big pinch of salt.

3 **roast the broccoli:** Slide the skillet into the oven and roast the broccoli until tender enough to slide a fork into the thicker stems, about 10 minutes. With oven mitts, move the pan back to the stovetop and reduce the oven temperature to 300°F (150°C), then tip the broccoli onto a plate.

4 **sauté the aromatics:** Put the skillet over medium heat, and add 2 tablespoons of the olive oil, the onion, and a pinch of salt. Cook the onion, stirring with the spatula, until lightly browned, 3 to 5 minutes. If the pan looks dry, add another tablespoon of olive oil. Toss in the garlic and red pepper flakes and cook, stirring, until the garlic is softened and has lost its raw smell, about 1 minute. Stir in the roasted broccoli.

5 **slow-bake the frittata:** Turn the heat under the skillet to medium-high. When it's actively sizzling, pour in the eggs and let cook for 30 seconds just to set the bottom. With oven mitts, slide the skillet into the oven and let the frittata cook until the eggs

continued

slow-baked broccoli frittata
continued

are just set, 20 to 25 minutes. The top will look lighter yellow, opaque, and firm, and you should be able to poke a table knife into the center, pull it out, and see no liquid egg on the blade. With the oven mitts, remove the pan from the oven, loosen the edges and bottom of the frittata with the spatula, and carefully ease it out onto a serving plate.

6 **eat**: Serve in wedges, warm or at room temperature. Just before serving, squeeze lemon juice over the top, drizzle with olive oil, and sprinkle with Parmigiano Reggiano to taste.

make ahead and store: Frittatas taste delicious at room temperature, so feel free to make this the day before, let cool to just-warm, slice into wedges, and store in the fridge on a serving plate covered tightly with reusable beeswax wrap or foil. Take the frittata out an hour or two before serving and garnish with the lemon, olive oil, and Parmesan. Leftovers can be refrigerated in a sealed container for up to a week and are great on a sandwich or green salad, at room temp or even cold.

Great with: A big green salad (page 182) and crispy-creamy potatoes (page 55).

the un-messy way to prep broccoli

If you just start chopping at a head of broccoli, you'll shear off tiny green buds along the way, leaving a mess on your cutting board (and marginally less broccoli to eat).

But if you slice through just the stalk and pull apart the florets with your hands as you go, they'll break more naturally and cleanly. The same is true of other cruciferous vegetables like cauliflower and bok choy. With napa cabbage, which has a core rather than a stalk, this technique can be helpful when making kimchi.

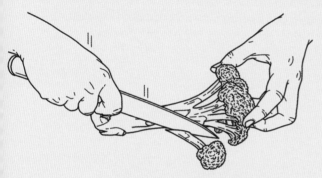

1) Slice off the outer florets

2) Chop off the rest of the crown (save the stem!)

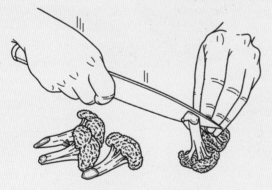

3) Cut florets to an even size—slice bigger ones just through the stalk . . .

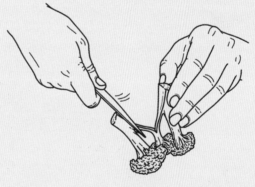

4) . . . then pull the florets apart by hand

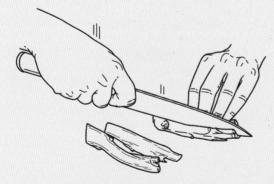

5) Trim the dry bottom from the stem and the tough skin off each side

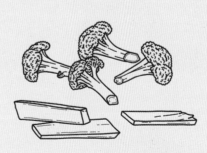

6) Slice the tender middle into sticks or coins about as thick as the florets

Heat the oven and whisk your eggs with salt and pepper as in step 1 on page 50, then . . .

Kuku Sabzi—an herby egg dish made for Nowruz, the Persian New Year—like *The New Persian Kitchen* author Louisa Shafia:

- Wash, dry well, and very finely chop 1½ bunches scallions and a mountain of cilantro and parsley—about 3 cups (60g) each, loosely packed before chopping. (Feel free to use a food processor—finer equals greener.)

- Sauté ¾ cup (85g) ground walnuts, 3 cloves minced garlic, and 3 teaspoons dried rose petals in the oil till fragrant in step 4.

- Stir in the scallions and herbs to wilt before adding a pinch of salt and pepper and the eggs in step 5.

Kimchi Shiitake like Mother-in-Law's Kimchi founder Lauryn Chun:

- Sauté 5 thinly sliced scallions and 15 thinly sliced shiitake mushroom caps in the oil in step 4 with a pinch of salt, till the mushrooms are soft.

- Stir in a heaping ¾ cup (125g) kimchi chopped into 1-inch (2.5cm) pieces before pouring in the eggs in step 5.

- Optionally, sprinkle on a couple teaspoons of gochugaru (Korean chile flakes) before baking.

Butternut Mash like *Start Simple* author Lukas Volger:

- Whisk 1 heaping cup (250g) leftover mashed roasted butternut squash 🥄 p. 199 and a few swipes of lemon zest and Parmesan from a Microplane into the eggs, too.

- Sauté 3 minced shallots along with a big pinch of dried thyme before pouring in the eggs in step 5.

CARAMELIZED CREAM SMASHED POTATOES

from aki kamozawa & h. alexander talbot

Aki and Alex, the duo behind Ideas in Food, discovered the benefits of frying all kinds of things in a thin layer of cream. You can also use leftover boiled potatoes, smash them as in step 1, and proceed with the recipe.

SERVES 4

1 pound (450g) baby potatoes

Salt

½ cup (120ml) heavy cream (or more as needed)

1 Bring the potatoes up to a gentle boil in a large pot of well-salted water (it should taste pleasantly salty) till a knife slides in easily, about 12 minutes. Drain in a colander, then let them cool till you can handle them. Smash each potato on a cutting board under a flat-bottomed plate to 1 inch (2.5cm) thick. Pour the cream into a large nonstick skillet. Sprinkle with a pinch of salt and add the potatoes in a single layer.

2 Turn the heat to medium. The cream will boil, steam, and separate into buttermilk and browning butter. When the bottoms of the potatoes are golden brown, flip them with a wide, nonmetal spatula to cook the other side. If the potatoes dry out before browning on both sides, add a little more cream. If the cream is too sloshy, turn up the heat and let it cook down till buttery and golden.

3 When brown and crisp on both sides, about 15 minutes total, lift the potatoes out with the spatula to a serving plate. Serve hot. To make ahead, keep the caramelized cream potatoes in a 200°F (95°C) oven on a sheet pan, uncovered, for up to 2 hours.

THE SHAKSHUKA THAT chef Sami Tamimi grew up eating for breakfast in Palestine looked little like the version more widely known today—his eggs weren't peeking up at him sunny-side, but rather scrambled into sauce-drunk ribbons. In this way, it has much in common with Turkish menemen and Yemeni shakshuka, both of which are simply scrambled, too.

Beyond being lush and comforting—the eggs now free to soak up the surrounding sauce—scrambling shakshuka is a boon to new cooks, perfectionists, and the yolk-phobic alike. There's no wondering if your yolks are done just so. Scrambled eggs practically shout when they're done, and, when simmering in a sauce this good, are incredibly resilient. They even stand up to reheating—so feel free to make too much.

Better still, you can make it almost entirely the day before—see the tips on page 58.

scrambled red shakshuka

from sami tamimi & tara wigley

SERVES 2 GENEROUSLY

MARINATED FETA

¼ cup (5g) flat-leaf parsley leaves

1½ teaspoons coriander seeds, divided

⅓ cup (45g) roughly crumbled feta

½ teaspoon Aleppo chile flakes (or ¼ teaspoon red pepper flakes)

3 tablespoons olive oil

SHAKSHUKA

1 yellow onion (150g)

3 garlic cloves

1 red bell pepper (140g)

½ teaspoon cumin seeds

20 ounces (575g) ripe tomatoes (about 5 Roma tomatoes)

2 tablespoons olive oil

1 teaspoon tomato paste

¼ teaspoon paprika

2 teaspoons harissa (preferably rose harissa)

⅓ cup (80ml) water

Fine sea salt and freshly ground black pepper

4 large eggs

1 **up to 2 days ahead, make the marinated feta:** On a cutting board with a chef's knife, roughly chop the parsley ☞ p. 258. In a small skillet, toast the coriander seeds until you can smell them, then roughly crush them with a mortar and pestle or skillet on the cutting board ☞ p. 59. In a small bowl with a spoon, stir together the feta, parsley, chile flakes, oil, and ½ teaspoon of the coriander seeds (save the rest for the shakshuka). Set aside until serving or refrigerate in a sealed container, if making ahead.

2 **prep the shakshuka ingredients:** Slice the onion about ¼ inch (6mm) thick ☞ p. 256 and mince the garlic cloves ☞ p. 257. Cut the bell pepper in half through the stem, pull out the seeds and stem, and slice ½ inch (1.3cm) thick. In the same small skillet used for the coriander, toast the cumin seeds until fragrant, then roughly crush them as you did the coriander seeds. Cut out the tough scar at the top of each tomato, then roughly chop the tomatoes. Line up all the other shakshuka ingredients by the stove.

3 **cook the sauce:** Heat the oil in a large skillet (with a lid or sheet pan nearby) over medium-high heat. Add the onion and cook, stirring occasionally with a wooden spoon, until softened and lightly browned, about 5 minutes. Add the bell pepper and cook until softened, another 5 minutes. Add the garlic, cumin, tomato paste, paprika, and remaining 1 teaspoon coriander. Cook until fragrant, another 1 minute, then add the tomatoes, harissa, water, ½ teaspoon fine sea salt, and a few grinds of black pepper. Continue to cook, uncovered, over medium heat, stirring occasionally, until the tomatoes have broken down and the sauce has thickened, about 15 minutes.

4 **just before serving, add the eggs:** Crack the eggs into a small bowl, add a pinch of salt and a few grinds of black pepper, and beat well with a fork. Slowly pour the eggs over the tomato mixture, then give the pan a couple of gentle stirs—you don't want the eggs to be too mixed in. Turn down the heat to medium-low, cover the pan, and let cook for 4 minutes. With oven mitts, lift the lid to check: The eggs should look light yellow, opaque, and firm throughout (like scrambled eggs).

continued

scrambled red shakshuka

continued

5 **eat**: Remove the pan from the heat, spoon the marinated feta over the top, sprinkle with a pinch of chile flakes, and serve at once.

make ahead and store: Both the marinated feta and the sauce for the shakshuka can be made through step 3 a day or two ahead of time and refrigerated in sealed containers. (They also scale up well, so feel free to double or triple either part of the recipe—the feta is lovely as a snack with crackers or spooned over roasted vegetables.) When ready to serve, reheat the sauce in the skillet and pick up from step 4. Even after scrambling in the eggs, the shakshuka holds up remarkably well in the fridge in a sealed container for 4 days. Reheat just until warmed through in the microwave or in a nonstick pan on the stovetop.

Great with: Soft pita and a platter of pretty sliced veg (bell peppers, radishes, cucumbers).

Once all is chopped, shakshuka happens fast ⤷

⌐ Just a couple of stirs (you want
  ⤷ ribbons of saucy eggs)

toast & grind spices (without a spice grinder)

Having an inexpensive coffee grinder can come in handy if you need to grind sturdy spices like cinnamon sticks and whole cardamom pods (and a mortar and pestle can handle the rest).

But even if you don't have either one, you can get the rich, fresh flavor and varied texture that come from toasting and grinding your own whole spices. Here's how.

1) Warm your spices in a small (dry) skillet over medium heat

2) Shake here and there till you can smell them

3a) Pour into a mortar . . .

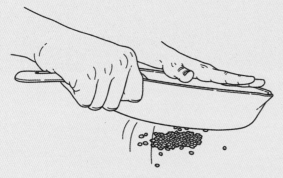

3b) . . . or onto a board—you can crush them with the bottom of the skillet (let it cool first)

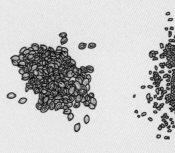

4) Crush as coarsely or finely as you like (finer = more flavor, but less texture)

2 brunch bells & whistles

A fruit salad that's just the hits. And a quenching Mexican agua fresca made from peanuts and two whole limes for bright, bittersweet complexity.

SERVES MANY

About ⅓ pound (150g) red fruit per person—cherries, plus any combination of plums, watermelon, strawberries, red grapes, and so on

RED FRUIT SALAD
from stacey rivera

1 Pit the cherries by squishing each with the side of a chef's knife on a cutting board, then pull out the pits (to avoid stains, wear a dark shirt and wash your cutting board quickly; lemon juice can help, even on your skin, and any lingering stains will fade over time).

2 Chop everything else bite-size. Stir it all, including the cherry juice, together with a serving spoon in a large bowl and serve (or chill the salad in a sealed container overnight, then take it out an hour or so ahead to bring it back to room temp to serve).

SERVES 6

2 juicy limes, rinsed, quartered, and any seeds flicked out

½ cup (55g) unsalted roasted peanuts

⅓ cup (65g) sugar

3 cups (715ml) water, divided

Ice

LIMONADA DE CACAHUATE
from roberto santibañez

1   No more than 1 hour before serving, blend the limes (yes, skins, too!), peanuts, sugar, and 2 cups (475ml) of the water with a blender or immersion blender till smooth, at least 1 minute.

2   Strain through a fine sieve (or colander lined with a clean kitchen towel) into a pitcher or other container, pressing on the pulp with a spatula to squeeze out the liquid. Toss the pulp or snack on it—it's tasty on buttered toast or yogurt but will get more bitter over time. Add the remaining 1 cup (240ml) water and stir well, then pour into ice-filled glasses and serve immediately.

good things to make ahead for lunches (& dinners & snacks) all week

IN THE INTEREST of being one step ahead of the cereal that stops fueling you halfway through the morning, the salads that aren't quite filling enough, and the sandwiches that lack heft, take a break on Sunday and make this riff on ajitsuke tamago, a Japanese ramen shop staple that will improve all kinds of meals.

This version comes from Momofuku Noodle Bar in New York City, where they boil the eggs very precisely (6 minutes and 50 seconds exactly) to hit that jammy yolk sweet spot—though you can tweak to your taste with the chart on page 66. They then soak the eggs in a soy marinade (more typically with the sweet Japanese rice wine mirin, but here with sherry vinegar and sugar) for a few hours. This step gives the eggs salt, sweetness, and tang, but mostly a lot of umami (aka the fifth taste, after salty, sour, sweet, and bitter, that's known for naturally making everything from soy sauce to anchovies to tomatoes more savory and delicious). Make as many as you want to eat in a week, which—you'll soon realize—is a lot.

soy sauce eggs
from momofuku

MAKES 6 EGGS

6 tablespoons (90ml) warm water

1 tablespoon sugar

2 tablespoons sherry vinegar

¾ cup (175ml) soy sauce*

6 large eggs, at refrigerator temperature

Ice

Maldon or other flaky salt, for serving

Freshly ground black pepper, for serving

1 **make the marinade:** In a medium bowl, whisk together the water and sugar until the sugar dissolves, then whisk in the sherry vinegar and soy sauce.

2 **boil the eggs:** Bring a large pot of water to a boil. Carefully lower the eggs into the boiling water with a slotted spoon (the eggs should be totally covered by the water) and set a timer for exactly 6 minutes and 50 seconds, stirring slowly for the first 1½ minutes to distribute the heat evenly. Meanwhile, fill a large bowl with cold water and plenty of ice to make an ice bath. When the timer goes off, scoop the eggs into the ice bath.

3 **peel:** Once the eggs are cool and the water isn't too icy for your hands, crack the eggs all over and peel them underwater ☞ p. 67.

4 **marinate:** Put your peeled eggs in the soy sauce mixture and marinate in the fridge for at least 2 hours or up to 6 hours, making sure they're completely submerged. If they're not covered with liquid, try a smaller, deeper bowl or set a small plate on top of the eggs to weigh them down. The longer they marinate, the more intense they'll get.

5 **eat:** Pull the eggs out of the marinade (but don't throw it out—you can use it for another round of eggs or to season other things like steamed rice or vegetables). When you're ready to eat, cut the eggs in half lengthwise with a paring knife and season with salt and pepper. Or halve them and warm in a bowl of soup, slice them into salads and sandwiches, mash them onto toast, and so on.

make ahead and store: The soy sauce eggs will keep, refrigerated in a sealed container, for a month.

Great with: Rice (page 105) and greens (page 208), sprinkled with some of the soy marinade.

*On Soy Sauces

Soy sauces vary a lot in intensity across styles and regions. If yours is on the saltier side (or you're not sure), aim for the shorter marinating time, then taste an egg to see if you want to keep brewing.

How Long Should I Boil (Yes, Boil) My Egg?

Some people will tell you that eggs cook more gently when you bring them up to a boil along with the water, then immediately shut off the heat (and, in this case, they should be called "hard-cooked" not "hard-boiled"). But if you miss the moment the water starts boiling, you have *no* idea how long the eggs need to cook. Plus, depending on the size and material of your pot, the water will heat faster or slower—making egg doneness very unpredictable.

Just straight-up boiling then cooling in ice water (like Momofuku does for its Soy Sauce Eggs on page 64) is much more precise and leaves you free *not* to stare at a pot, waiting for it to boil. Bonus: Eggs started in boiling water are easier to peel.

Here's how long to actually boil large eggs from the fridge to get the kind you want.

5 MINUTES AND UNDER

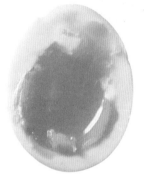

very runny
(more of a coddled egg, better
for blending into dressings)

6 MINUTES

soft-boiled

6:50 MINUTES

Momofuku "jammy"

8 MINUTES

medium-boiled
(or firmer jammy)

11 MINUTES

hard-boiled

12 MINUTES AND OVER

beyond this point, things start to
get chalky and rubbery

the easiest way to peel eggs
(whether you're marinating them or not)

No method will release every hard-boiled egg from its shell without fail (especially if the eggs are super fresh), but this trick gives you the best odds of smooth eggs without struggle, as the water rushes in to help loosen the shell *almost* every time.

1) Tap and roll to crackle
the shell all over

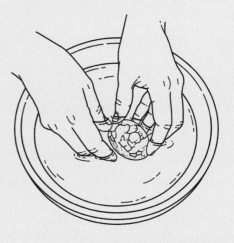

2) Plunge into a big bowl of water

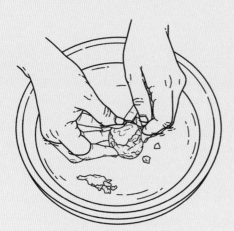

3) Start pulling away the
peel at the fatter end, where
there's an air pocket

4) Look how smooth!

THIS RECIPE FROM Nopalito chef and owner Gonzalo Guzmán breaks every one of the most discouraging rules about cooking beans from scratch—that you have to soak them overnight, only add salt at the end, and hang out skimming away so-called impurities while they cook. He even kicks off the pot with a little apple cider vinegar, proving that, while it's true acidic ingredients can keep beans from softening, a couple spoonfuls of vinegar (or lemon halves or chopped tomatoes) won't utterly ruin them. He also harnesses the best shortcut for maintaining an even simmer (and tenderly cooked beans): Stick them in the oven instead of babysitting them on the stove.

Here, the beans start with softened chile and onion, but Gonzalo's method can become your go-to for most any bean, even when you skip that step (see more flavoring ideas on page 71). The best part about realizing these rules are flexible is that it puts comforting, inexpensive, choose-your-own-adventure beans in reach within a couple of hours any day you feel like cooking them. In fact, Gonzalo's recipe saves us from the worst thing we do to beans: *not* cook them. The longer we ignore them in the pantry, dried beans get more grizzled and harder to cook—but that shouldn't be a problem anymore.

frijoles negros de la olla

from gonzalo guzmán

MAKES 6 CUPS (1.4L)

1 pound (450g) dried black beans (scant 3 cups)

2 tablespoons neutral oil, such as canola

½ white onion, chopped
⚶ p. 256

1 small jalapeño chile, chopped ⚶ p. 70

2 tablespoons apple cider vinegar

10 cups (2.4L) water

1½ teaspoons fine sea salt

1 **sizzle the aromatics:** Heat the oven to 350°F (175°C). Pour the beans into a bowl to scan for any pebbles—they're rare, but you don't want any sneaking through. In a large ovenproof pot with a lid nearby, heat the oil over medium-high heat. Add the onion and jalapeño, lower the heat to medium, and cook, stirring occasionally with a wooden spoon, until the onion is soft and translucent, about 5 minutes. Add the vinegar and let it simmer until about half is evaporated, about 1 minute. (The sharp, spicy steam might make you cough—crack a window or turn on the fan if so.)

2 **simmer the beans and eat:** Add the beans, water, and salt to the pot and bring to a boil over high heat. Cover the pot and, with oven mitts, carefully set the pot in the center of the oven. (Alternatively, to cook on the stovetop, reduce the heat to a low simmer, cover, and check on them more often to make sure they're simmering gently.) Cook the beans until tender and creamy—set a timer and start checking after an hour, as fresher beans will cook faster, and check more often as the beans get closer to done (this can take 2 to 3 hours for older beans). If the liquid drops below the level of the beans before they're tender, add enough water to fully submerge them again. When they start to seem soft enough, taste 5 beans. When they're done, they will all be soft, with no grittiness remaining. Adjust the seasoning to taste and serve at any temperature you like.

make ahead and store: Let the beans cool till you can comfortably handle the pot, no more than 2 hours, and store them in their cooking liquid, tightly sealed, in the fridge (I do this right in the covered pot). They'll keep well for about 5 days, or freeze well for about 3 months ⚶ p. 250. Reheat in the microwave or a pot on the stovetop with a bit of their liquid, stirring occasionally.

Great with: Queso fresco, cilantro, and warm tortillas.

HOW TO
handle hot chiles without spicy surprises

Most of the spiciness of your average hot chile—from a compound known as capsaicin—is nestled in the white ribs that line its belly, not in the seeds. Capsaicin makes food deliciously hot but can also sting any body parts it touches along the way (hands, eyes, other sensitive bits).

There's no shame in wearing gloves (or tucking your hand inside a plastic baggie or even a large scrap of onion peel) to protect your hands, and this slicing method from cookbook author and chef Roberto Santibañez might be the tidiest way to not feel the burn. (If you want zero seeds or ribs, you can halve the pepper lengthwise and scrape out the innards with a spoon first—just take care not to touch anything they've rubbed against.)

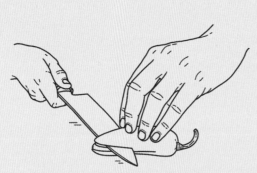

1) Carefully make horizontal slices, leaving the stem end intact

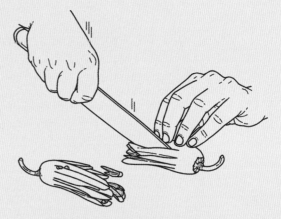

2) Slice vertically, still keeping the stem end intact

3) Slice vertically again, crosswise, to chop the pepper into bits, seeds and all

4) Sniff the chile—if it stings your nose a little, it's a spicy one

Scrape in as much chile as you like (based on the spiciness sniff test), then wash the board, knife, and your hands!

the no-soak, no-rules pot of beans

salt (yes, at the beginning)

good-tasting aromatics, whatever you have and feel like

dried (not soaked) beans

water to cover the beans by a couple inches (5cm)

This is really all it takes to cook dried beans from scratch anytime you feel like it. Put everything you see here in a pot and simmer it gently, on the stovetop or in the oven. That's it. Per food writer Tamar Adler, once you taste five creamy beans with no chalkiness remaining, you're set.

This bare-bones template comes from Gonzalo Guzmán's Frijoles Negros de la Olla (page 68) but you can flavor it however you want. For Brazilian black-eyed peas, *Gran Cocina Latina* author Dr. Maricel E. Presilla tosses in scallions, cilantro sprigs, and a small peeled, halved onion. For Tuscan cannellini beans, *Guardian* columnist Rachel Roddy adds fresh sage, lots of olive oil, and a few unpeeled garlic cloves, then squeezes the soft poached garlic into the broth at the end. Chef Patch Troffer goes with coriander seed, a lot of oregano, a little mint, and a lemon, halved and charred cut-side down in a hot, dry skillet, plus more of the herbs and a splash of sherry vinegar at the end.

How Long Different Beans Take to Simmer, Give or Take*

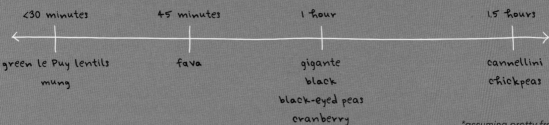

<30 minutes	45 minutes	1 hour	1.5 hours
green le Puy lentils	fava	gigante	cannellini
mung		black	chickpeas
		black-eyed peas	
		cranberry	

*assuming pretty fresh beans in a 350°F (175°C) oven—but beans will vary so check early (more trouble-shooting tips on page 74).

CRISPY BLACK-EYED PEA HUMMUS
from jerrelle guy

In her cookbook *Black Girl Baking*, Jerrelle Guy pulls the texture of hummus to extremes, using creamy black-eyed peas in place of the chickpeas traditionally used in the Middle East, and pulling out a scoop of the beans to roast crisp while blending the rest smooth.

SERVES 2 TO 4

1¾ cups (325g) drained, home-cooked or canned black-eyed peas, divided 🍵 p. 71

¼ cup (60ml) olive oil, plus more for drizzling

Salt

1 head garlic

¼ cup (60g) well-stirred tahini

¼ cup (60ml) lemon juice 🍵 p. 203

2 tablespoons water

1 teaspoon ground cumin

1 Heat the oven to 400°F (200°C) and line a sheet pan with parchment paper

2 Spread 3 tablespoons of the black-eyed peas on the sheet pan. Sprinkle with a little olive oil and salt. On a cutting board with a serrated knife, slice the top ½ inch (1.3cm) off the garlic head to expose the cloves, sprinkle with olive oil and salt, and bundle in foil. Add to the sheet pan and roast together in the oven until the peas are crispy, 25 to 30 minutes.

3 With oven mitts, take the pan out of the oven. Let the garlic cool, then squeeze out the softened cloves. With a blender or immersion blender, combine the garlic cloves, the remaining drained peas, ¼ cup (60ml) olive oil, the tahini, lemon juice, water, cumin, and a pinch of salt. Blend until smooth, scraping down the sides with a silicone spatula as needed. Taste and adjust the seasoning.

4 To serve, scrape the hummus into a serving bowl and top with the crispy black-eyed peas and a drizzle of olive oil.

Any time you have a pot of beans (page 71), you can make . . .

Frijoles Refritos like Nopalito chef Gonzalo Guzmán:

- Fry 3 tablespoons finely chopped white onion in ½ cup (120ml) neutral oil till deep golden brown.

- Add 3 cups (510g) warm beans, 1½ cups (355ml) bean cooking liquid, and ¾ teaspoon dried oregano.

- Mash with a potato masher or large serving fork till slightly chunky, adding water if it gets dry. Serve hot.

Beans on Garlic Toast like *New York Times* restaurant critic Tejal Rao:

- Brush both sides of a slice of crusty sourdough with olive oil and broil on a sheet pan about 4 inches (10cm) from the heat, flipping once, till golden.

- Gently scrape a garlic clove all over one side of the hot toast. Set the garlic toast in a shallow bowl and ladle over plenty of hot beans and bean broth.

- Top with olive oil, chopped herbs, flaky salt, grated Parmesan, and black pepper.

Armenian Bean Noodle Soup like *Lavash* authors Ara Zada & Kate Leahy:

- Sauté a chopped yellow onion in 2 tablespoons butter, add 2 chopped Yukon gold potatoes, then add 6 cups (1.4L) bean cooking broth or water and simmer for 5 minutes.

- Add 3 cups (510g) cooked beans and ½ cup (60g) broken vermicelli or angel hair pasta and simmer till the noodles are cooked through and potatoes fork-tender, about 10 more minutes.

- Top with chopped cilantro and dill to serve.

common dried bean woes
(& how to fix them)

Great news: From-scratch beans are very forgiving and fixable.
Here are some handy ways to manipulate them.

the beans cooked forever and still didn't get soft.

THIS TIME

Keep simmering while you make a speedy backup dinner (page 97). If they're not making progress after three hours, thank them and put them in the compost.

NEXT TIME

Don't let beans hang around your pantry for more than two years (and buy from shops that keep their stocks moving—if the package is dusty or faded, it's a bad sign). Dial back any acidic ingredients.

they're all mushy and broken apart.

THIS TIME

Consider rebranding—*Washington Post* writer Aaron Hutcherson actually prefers the extra creaminess of semi-broken-down beans. If you don't, blend them into a smooth soup or hummus (page 72).

NEXT TIME

Go for the gentler simmer of the oven versus the stovetop, and check them often toward the end of cooking.

they're awfully bland.

THIS TIME

Add a little more salt, but know that it will need time to soak in. And dress up the beans as you go: a little lemon juice or vinegar, olive oil, salt, and pepper are often all you'll need.

NEXT TIME

Throw in any aromatics you have lying around (see ideas on page 71—no need to sauté first) at the beginning, plus a bit more salt.

they're *too* salty.

THIS TIME

Dilute the cooking liquid with a little water (the salt will keep ebbing back into the liquid through osmosis in time). In the meantime, un-salted dressings!

NEXT TIME

Salt judiciously at the beginning and taste the broth as you go (even if the beans aren't ready)—if it's too salty, your beans will be, too.

uh-oh, they're so spicy.

THIS TIME

Serve with lots of sour cream or crema. Other bright flavors, like lime, can also be good distractions. The same diluting with water trick (from the salty woe above) can work here, too.

NEXT TIME

Sniff the chile as you're chopping (see page 70) to get a sense of how spicy it is, and use less if the vapors are stinging your nose.

LENTILS FOLDED INTO YOGURT, SPINACH & BASIL
from peter miller

Green lentils are like quicker-cooking beans—taking as little as 25 minutes, just in time for dinner tonight. Here, Peter Miller, Seattle bookstore owner and author of *Lunch at the Shop*, turns them into a thoughtful lunch as well. It's as totable as tuna salad, but bound with bright yogurt rather than mayo, among other sprightly additions.

SERVES 4

½ cup (60g) chopped walnuts

2 cups (60g) baby spinach

1 cup (20g) fresh basil leaves

1 cup (150g) cooked small green le Puy lentils 👐 p. 71

2 tablespoons fresh flat-leaf parsley leaves, chopped 👐 p. 258

1 garlic clove, finely chopped 👐 p. 257

1½ lemons, divided

1 cup (240ml) Greek yogurt

¼ cup (60ml) olive oil

Salt and freshly ground black pepper

Buttered toast or lettuce, for serving

½ cup (50g) Parmesan cheese shaved with a vegetable peeler

1 In a small sauté pan over medium heat, toast the walnuts, stirring with a silicone spatula, until golden, 5 to 7 minutes. Tear the spinach and basil into bite-size pieces.

2 Place the lentils in a large bowl and mix in the spinach, basil, parsley, and garlic. Squeeze in the juice of 1 lemon 👐 p. 203, stir, then fold in the yogurt. Slowly pour in the oil, stirring, to combine. Taste and season with salt and pepper. Fold in the toasted nuts, and finish with a drizzle of oil. Eat now, or save for lunch tomorrow. (The lentils will keep in an airtight jar or container in the refrigerator for 3 days.)

3 Bring the lentils close to room temperature before serving. Serve with a slice of buttered toast or on a lettuce leaf as a salad. Top with a squeeze of lemon juice, some Parmesan, and a grind of fresh pepper.

ONE OF THE most revelatory and widely loved techniques from *Salt Fat Acid Heat*, Samin Nosrat's cookbook and TV show full of revelatory and widely loved techniques, has only three ingredients and a method that can be summed up as follows: Soak in buttermilk overnight—just as Southern cooks do for fried chicken—then, instead, roast.

And yet, bundled up in Samin's straight-shooting method are all four of the tenets of her famed curriculum: *Salt* in the marinade sinks deep into the chicken to season it through and through, realigning the proteins to help it hold onto its juices as it heats in the oven, instead of squeezing them out. *Fat* in the buttermilk and chicken itself (as well as the buttermilk's natural sugars) give the chicken its signature handsomely lacquered skin. Lactic *acid* in the buttermilk further tenderizes the proteins and infuses gentle tang. And *heat*, concentrated more at the back and sides of the oven, helps the slower-to-cook legs of the chicken keep up with the breast. What all of this means: really good roast chicken that's really hard to overcook.

There is just one more ingredient: time. Start marinating tonight for the juiciest chicken tomorrow, seasoned down to the bone. And for the times you're feeling less patient (or less prepared), see page 82.

buttermilk-marinated roast chicken (aka chicken for tomorrow)
from samin nosrat

SERVES 4

One 3½- to 4-pound (1.6 to 1.8kg) chicken

Fine sea salt

2 cups (475ml) buttermilk

1   **the day before you want chicken, prep the bird**: Set the chicken on a rimmed sheet pan. If there's a bag of giblets tucked inside the chicken, be sure to pull it out.* Cut off the pointy wingtips by slicing through the first wing joint with kitchen shears or a sharp knife (so they don't burn—save them for stock 🥄 p. 81). Season the chicken inside and out with 1 tablespoon of salt total and let it sit for 30 minutes.

2   **make the marinade**: In a large bowl, combine 4 teaspoons salt and the buttermilk and stir with a spoon to dissolve the salt. Lift the chicken into a gallon-size (3.8L) resealable plastic bag and pour in the buttermilk. If the chicken looks like it won't fit in a gallon-size bag, use a larger resealable bag or double up two larger plastic produce bags to prevent leakage and tie the bag with a piece of twine. If you have no bags that will work, use a bowl and cover it tightly, but you'll want to turn the chicken a few times to make sure it all gets access to the marinade.

3   Seal the bag, squish the buttermilk around the chicken, place on a rimmed plate, and refrigerate for 12 to 24 hours. If you remember, turn the bag partway through marinating so every part of the chicken gets marinated, but it's not essential.

4   **about 2 hours and 15 minutes before you want to eat, get ready to roast**: Take the chicken bundle out of the fridge and leave on the counter for 1 hour to lose some chill. Heat the oven to 425°F (220°C) with a rack in the center.

continued

*About Those Bits

Those bits you stumbled on inside your chicken? You can cook with them! Easiest might be tossing the heart, gizzard, and neck into the no-fuss stock on page 81 (leave out liver—the darkest, flattest bit—as it tends to take over). They also freeze well, tightly sealed, for 3 to 4 months for other recipes.

5   **just before roasting, ready the chicken**: Find a 10-inch (25cm) cast-iron skillet or shallow roasting pan. Remove the chicken from the plastic bag, scraping off as much buttermilk with your fingers as you reasonably can. Set the chicken in the pan, breast-side up 🥄 p. 77. Tightly tie the legs of the chicken together with a piece of kitchen twine.

6   **start roasting**: Set the pan in the oven on the center rack and slide the pan all the way to the back. Turn the pan so the chicken legs are pointing toward the back left corner and the breast is pointing toward the center of the oven (the back corners are usually the hottest spots in the oven, so this positioning will help keep the breast from overcooking before the legs are done). Close the oven—the chicken should start sizzling soon.

7   **turn the pan**: After the chicken starts to brown, about 20 minutes, turn down the heat to 400°F (200°C). Roast for another 10 minutes, then use oven mitts to turn the pan so the legs are facing the back right corner of the oven.

8   **finish roasting and eat**: Continue cooking until the chicken is beautifully browned all over and, when you insert a knife down to the bone between the leg and the thigh, the meat looks firm and pale, not squishy and pink 🥄 p. 170, and the juices run clear, about 30 minutes more (an instant-read thermometer will register 165°F (74°C) in the thickest part of the thigh and breast). Using tongs, lift the chicken to a cutting board (preferably with a groove to catch any juices) or platter and let it rest for 10 minutes before carving 🥄 p. 80 with a sharp knife and serving.

store: Roast chicken, tightly sealed in the refrigerator, makes excellent leftovers. You can either carve or pull off all the meat so it's easier to use throughout the week, or stick the whole bird on a plate and cover it with a reusable beeswax wrap or plastic wrap for 4 days, or freeze in an airtight container 🥄 p. 250 for 4 months. Eat it cold, warm, or hot, in sandwiches, soups, grain bowls, tacos, and more.

Great with: Chiles toreados (page 79) and mayo in a warm tortilla.

CHILES TOREADOS
from roberto santibañez

In his cookbook *Tacos, Tortas, and Tamales*, Roberto Santibañez gives us one of his favorite tacos to make at home: warm tortillas smeared with mayonnaise, filled with pulled roast chicken and this fiery, super-savory condiment served in Japanese restaurants in Mexico City.

MAKES 4 TO 6 SERVINGS

12 fresh serrano or very small jalapeño chiles

1½ tablespoons olive or canola oil

1 medium white onion, sliced into half-moons ¼ inch (6mm) thick 🌿 p. 256

⅛ teaspoon fine sea salt

2 tablespoons Worcestershire sauce

A scant 2 tablespoons soy sauce

¼ cup (60ml) lime juice (from 2 juicy limes), plus more to taste 🌿 p. 203

1 Heat a large skillet over medium heat till hot but not smoking. Meanwhile, firmly roll each chile between your palms for a few seconds without breaking it. Add the chiles to the pan and cook, turning occasionally with tongs, until blackened in spots, 10 to 15 minutes.

2 Transfer the chiles to a bowl. Add the oil, onion, and salt to the pan and cook, stirring with a wooden spoon, until the onion is soft and golden brown at the edges, about 5 minutes. Turn off the heat, return the chiles to the pan, and poke each chile once with the tip of a sharp knife to release a little juice. Add the Worcestershire sauce, soy sauce, and lime juice and stir well.

3 Transfer the chiles, onions, and all of the juices to the bowl. (If you want it even spicier, pull out the chiles, roughly chop, and stir back in.) Let sit for at least 5 minutes. Season to taste with more salt and lime. Chiles toreados keep well in a sealed container in the refrigerator for 3 days.

HOW TO
be really relaxed about carving a chicken
(& make bonus stock)

The first thing to know as you stare down a roast chicken is that you *will* find your way. There are natural places to slide your knife through at the joints, and even confident home cooks have to feel around with their hands sometimes to find them. Don't worry about doing it perfectly—you can pull off every little bit of meat left behind after your first pass.

TO CARVE:

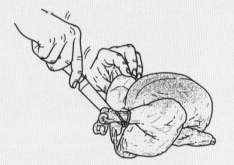

1) Cut away twine at the ankles with a paring knife if you've trussed

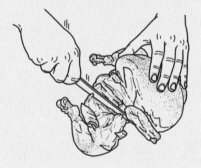

2) Slice at the hip, pull open the leg till the joint is free, then finish slicing through

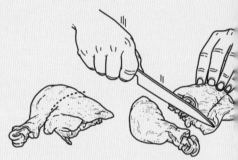

3) Cut the thigh and drumstick apart—double the servings!

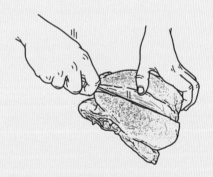

4) Start slicing away each breast by scraping down following the rib cage

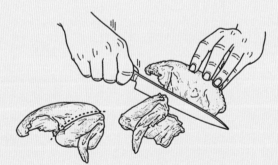

5) Slice through the wing joint

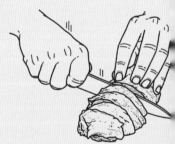

6) Slice the breast in thick slices crosswise against the grain of the meat

7) Pull all extra meat off the carcass, and don't miss the back!

This is also the perfect moment to habitually make chicken stock. You don't need a recipe or to gather up a huge pile of bones that you will definitely forget about in your freezer. Just simmer a mini batch while you eat dinner and do other things, and whatever's in the pot will taste a million times fresher than something out of a box (plus, it comes free with the chicken).

TO MAKE STOCK:

1) Throw the carcass and any other leftover bones into a pot

2) Cover with water and toss in a bay leaf or veg trimmings like onion scraps if you have them (or don't)

3) Simmer gently on the stovetop—let it go as long as you have time for (an hour or two is good)

4) Cool till no longer hot (no more than 2 hours), then strain, seal, and refrigerate for 4 days, or freeze for 3 months

LIKE A GOOD rotisserie bird from the grocery store, slow-roasting a chicken lets both the white and dark meat turn buttery-soft enough to pull from the bone instead of formally carving. And, unlike with high-heat roasting, which races from juicy to parched if you don't catch it in time (or have a buttermilk marinade as insurance, see page 76), you can be much more leisurely, without disaster.

Now, about that skin: Roasted low and slow, it won't get crispy. This is why, in food editor Lindsay Maitland Hunt's cookbook *Help Yourself*, after slow-roasting a whole chicken, she tugs off all the skin and blasts it at high heat. Each yanked-off piece becomes a practically fried chicken chip you can sprinkle over your juicy pulled chicken and into your mouth.

slow-roasted chicken with extra-crisp skin (aka chicken for today)
from lindsay maitland hunt

SERVES 4 TO 6

One 4-pound (1.8kg) whole chicken

¾ teaspoon fine sea salt

Freshly ground black pepper

1 lemon, quartered, plus more wedges for serving

1 large sprig fresh rosemary

1 tablespoon chopped fresh parsley leaves
🍵 p. 258

Flaky sea salt, for serving

1 **about 3½ hours before you want chicken, get ready to roast**: Heat your oven to 300°F (150°C) with a rack in the center. Set the chicken on a rimmed sheet pan or large skillet and pat it dry with paper towels. If there's a bag of giblets tucked inside the chicken, pull it out 🍵 p. 76. Sprinkle the chicken all over with the fine sea salt and generous grinds of pepper (to keep from getting chickeny hands everywhere, pre-grind a little pile of pepper and use one hand to hold the chicken and the other to season). Finish with the chicken breast-side up in the pan 🍵 p. 77 and stuff the quartered lemon and rosemary inside the cavity.

2 **slow-roast the chicken**: Slide the pan into the center of the oven and roast until an instant-read thermometer in the thickest part of the thigh registers 165°F (74°C), 2 to 3 hours 🍵 p. 170. With oven mitts, take the pan out of the oven and set it on a cool section of the stovetop to cool slightly. Crank the oven up to 425°F (220°C).

3 **crisp the skin**: Pull the skin off the entire chicken, using a paring knife to free any parts that stick (don't stress about parts that are really stuck, like the wings—just eat those as is). If it's too hot to touch, use tongs to help. Lay all the skin on a clean rimmed sheet pan. Roast the chicken skin in the oven until deep golden brown and crispy, 10 to 15 minutes, then use oven mitts to move the pan to a cool section of the stovetop.

4 **carve**: While the skin roasts, carve 🍵 p. 80 or pull the meat off the bones—it should be very easy to pull apart—and set on a serving plate. Save the bones for stock 🍵 p. 81. Pour off any pan juices into a small bowl, and cover to keep warm.

5 **crumble the crispy skin and eat**: When the skin is cool enough to touch, crumble it over the chicken and drizzle with juices from both pans. Sprinkle with the parsley, a few grinds of pepper, and a pinch of flaky sea salt. Serve with lemon wedges.

make ahead and store: Leftovers will keep in a sealed container in the refrigerator for 4 days to work into meals throughout the week or in the freezer for 4 months 🍵 p. 250. Lindsay recommends eating all the chicken skin right now.

Great with: Farro (page 87) and skillet scallions (page 209).

IN HER COOKBOOK *Smitten Kitchen Every Day*, Deb Perelman makes a case for grain salads "where the grain is the minority ingredient, not just a foundation that vegetables are dotted across as an afterthought." A grain can be a salad ingredient like any other, rather than the overstuffed bed.

In this slaw, the farro is scattered through to poke up here and there "like nubby crouton accents," as Perelman says, providing just enough texture to give your teeth a place to pause, and just enough heft to make slaw a meal. And of course, this means that if you make a big batch of farro—or other whole grains like freekeh or spelt, or a mix (page 87)—you can sprinkle them like the croutons they deserve to be, all through the week.

winter slaw with farro
from deb perelman

SERVES 6 TO 8

½ cup (100g) finely chopped dried apricots

¼ cup (60ml) white wine vinegar

1 medium (2 pounds/900g) head green cabbage

1⅓ cups (145g) cooked farro, cooled (from about ¾ cup uncooked) 👁 p. 87

⅓ cup (45g) roughly chopped well-toasted almonds 👁 p. 261

2 ounces (55g) Parmesan, thinly shaved on a grater or with a vegetable peeler

3 tablespoons olive oil

¼ teaspoon fine sea salt

Freshly ground black pepper

1 **prep everything**: In a small bowl, combine the apricots with the vinegar and set aside while preparing the other ingredients.

2 On a large cutting board with a chef's knife, cut the cabbage in half and slice out the core (and eat the core as a crunchy snack); then cut the halves again so you have quarters. Slice the cabbage into very thin ribbons. You'll have about 12 cups (2.8L) total, which will seem like too much, but it will wilt down with dressing on it. Pile it into your biggest bowl.

3 **toss the slaw**: Add to the bowl the apricots and their soaking vinegar, the farro, almonds, and most of the Parmesan, plus the olive oil, salt, and several turns of freshly ground pepper. Toss with a large serving spoon or salad tossers to combine. Give it 15 minutes to let the ingredients settle before making seasoning adjustments.

4 **rest and eat**: After 15 minutes, taste and add more vinegar, Parmesan, oil, salt, and pepper as needed. Scoop the slaw onto plates and top with the remaining Parmesan.

make ahead and store: The slaw's textures are best for serving to company today but will keep for a few days in the fridge tightly sealed for great take-to-work lunches.

FARRO & OLIVE SALAD
from heidi swanson

In this famously electric grain salad from Heidi Swanson's cookbook *Near & Far*, everything should be chopped about the size of the farro so you can spoon it up uninterrupted. Like the slaw on page 84, this salad makes boiled farro sparkle, but the toasting technique on page 87 brings out even more charm.

SERVES 6

1 pound (450g) pitted green olives (preferably Castelvetrano), rinsed and coarsely chopped

¼ cup (60ml) extra-virgin olive oil

1 cup (90g) chopped toasted walnuts ☙ p. 261

4 to 6 scallions, trimmed and chopped ☙ p. 137

1 bunch chives, minced ☙ p. 258

Scant ½ teaspoon red pepper flakes

1 tablespoon honey

2 tablespoons freshly squeezed lemon juice ☙ p. 203

⅓ cup (70g) golden raisins, chopped

½ teaspoon fine sea salt

2½ cups (400g) cooked farro, cooled (from 1¼ cups uncooked) ☙ p. 87

Pecorino Romano, for serving

1 In a medium bowl with a wooden spoon, stir together the olives, olive oil, walnuts, scallions, chives, red pepper flakes, honey, lemon juice, raisins, and salt. Set aside (or refrigerate, tightly sealed) until ready to serve the salad.

2 If you've refrigerated the olive mix or the farro, set them out for 30 minutes before tossing them together. Taste and tweak the salt or lemon juice if needed. Serve topped with thin shavings of Pecorino Romano from a vegetable peeler.

Mix a few grains that have similar cook times

Maria likes boiling in half broth, half water (or all water)

Toast the grains (if you want them to taste nutty) with flavor-boosters

the extra-easy, extra-delicious way to make a pot of grains

While you can always follow the package instructions for whole grains like farro or quinoa, what they don't tell you is *you don't have to*: As Maria Speck breaks down in *Simply Ancient Grains*, you can boil most grains just like pasta (bonus: you won't have to worry about accidentally scorching the bottom of the pot). The only grains Maria doesn't recommend cooking this way are the tiniest ones that would melt right through a strainer.

All you need is a big pot, lots of happily boiling water (covering the grains by at least 3 inches/7.5cm), and enough salt to season them well as they cook. But this is also your chance to play. Maria mix-and-matches a few grains with similar cook times (see the timing chart below), sometimes toasting them first in the dry pot till they smell nutty, along with whole spices or chiles. And she amps up the water with half broth—enough to round it out, without overtaking the goodness of the grain itself.

How Long Different grains Take to Boil, give or Take*

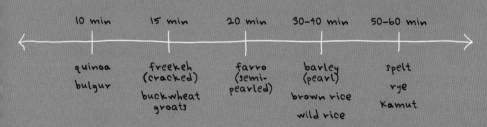

10 min	15 min	20 min	30–40 min	50–60 min
quinoa bulgur	freekeh (cracked) buckwheat groats	farro (semi-pearled)	barley (pearl) brown rice wild rice	spelt rye Kamut

*depending on your grains (older ones will take longer) and personal preference—Maria likes when some of the grains have popped open, for a mix of chew and soft

WHEN MUCH OF the world was tending—and in many cases, soon abandoning—their first sourdough starter, a savvy cult started to develop around a much lower-maintenance bread recipe. For the "Basically Guide to Better Baking," *Bon Appétit* senior editor Sarah Jampel developed the recipe whose name says it all, the one that would get people who'd never bought a packet of yeast plunging their fingers into glossy dough and pulling their very own rippling, bronzed sheets of focaccia from the oven, impressing everyone around them, but mostly themselves.

There is no kneading, no bread-baking terminology or special equipment (though there is a cool trick involving forks in step 4 that Sarah learned from *Bread Toast Crumbs* author Alexandra Stafford), no doing much of anything other than waiting and ushering dough from one olive oil–puddled vessel to another. Maybe even more than the sourdough, this cult stuck. Join them.

shockingly easy no-knead focaccia
from sarah jampel

SERVES 10 TO 12

1 (¼-ounce/7g) envelope active dry yeast (about 2¼ teaspoons)

2 teaspoons honey

2½ cups (590ml) lukewarm water

5 cups (625g) all-purpose flour 🥄 p. 215

2½ teaspoons fine sea salt

¼ cup plus 2 tablespoons (90ml) extra-virgin olive oil, divided, plus more for your hands

¼ cup (60g) unsalted butter (optional), plus more for the pan

Flaky sea salt, for topping

2 to 4 garlic cloves, peeled (optional) 🥄 p. 257

1 **ideally 1 day or at least 8½ hours before you want focaccia, test your yeast**: In a medium bowl, whisk together the yeast, honey, and water and let sit for 5 minutes. You'll know your yeast is alive and well if it foams or looks creamy—if not, start over with new yeast (check the expiration date).

2 **mix the dough**: Add the flour and fine sea salt and stir with a silicone spatula until you have a shaggy dough with no floury streaks. Pour ¼ cup (60ml) of the olive oil into a large bowl that will fit in your refrigerator. Scrape the dough into the bowl and flip to coat it in oil.

3 **let it slow-rise in the fridge**: Cover with a silicone lid or plastic wrap and chill until the dough is doubled in size (it should look very bubbly), at least 8 hours and up to 1 day. Or if you're in a rush, let it rise at room temperature until doubled in size, 3 to 4 hours.

4 **at least 4½ hours before you want focaccia, let it rise in the pan**: Generously butter a 9 by 13-inch (23 by 33cm) cake pan for thicker, puffier focaccia, or a 13 by 18-inch (33 by 45cm) rimmed sheet pan for thinner, crispier focaccia. Pour 1 tablespoon of the olive oil into the center of the pan. Keeping the dough in the bowl and using two forks, lift the edge of the dough farthest from you up and over into the center of the bowl 🥄 p. 92. Give the bowl a quarter turn and repeat. Do this two more times to deflate the dough and form it into a rough ball. Scrape the dough into the prepared pan. Pour in any oil left in the bowl and flip the dough to coat. Let it rise, uncovered, in a dry, warm spot (near a radiator or on top of your refrigerator) until doubled in size, at least 1½ hours and up to 4 hours.

continued

5 **bake the focaccia**: Heat the oven to 450°F (230°C) with a rack in the center. To see if the dough is ready, poke it with your finger. It should spring back slowly, leaving a small visible hole. If it springs back quickly, the dough isn't ready. (If at this point the dough is ready to bake but you aren't, you can chill it for up to 1 hour.) Lightly oil your hands and, if needed, gently stretch the dough to fill the pan (you will probably need to do this only with the sheet pan version). Dimple the focaccia all over with your fingers, as if you were playing the piano, pressing your fingers all the way to the bottom of the pan. Drizzle with the remaining 1 tablespoon olive oil and sprinkle lightly with flaky sea salt. Bake until the focaccia is puffed and golden brown all over, 20 to 30 minutes.

6 **(optionally) paint it with garlic butter just before serving**: In a small saucepan over medium heat, melt the butter, then turn off the heat and slide the saucepan to a cool part of the stove. Grate in the garlic cloves with a Microplane. Return the saucepan to medium heat and cook, stirring often with a wooden spoon, until the garlic is just lightly toasted, 30 to 45 seconds. (Or, if you prefer spicy raw garlic to mellower toasted garlic, you can grate the garlic into the hot butter, off the heat, then brush it on right away.) With a pastry brush (preferably) or spoon, brush the garlic butter all over the focaccia and slice into squares or rectangles.

make ahead and store: Focaccia is best the day it's made but still delicious for a couple of days, especially if toasted. It also keeps well in the freezer: Slice it into pieces, store it in a freezer-safe container for up to 3 months, then warm it up on a sheet pan in a 300°F (150°C) oven.

Great with: Sliced ripe tomatoes and mayonnaise d'avocat (page 91).

MAYONNAISE D'AVOCAT
from dr. jessica b. harris

This airy spread from the islands of Guadeloupe is "the perfect solution to too many ripening avocados when you're sick of guacamole," culinary historian Dr. Jessica B. Harris writes in her book *Iron Pots & Wooden Spoons.* It also takes away the anxiety of making (and breaking) your own mayonnaise—the oil absorbs right into the avocado, smoothing and fluffing as it goes.

SERVES 2 TO 3

1 very ripe avocado

1 small fresh habanero chile, seeded and minced p. 70

1 sprig parsley, minced p. 258

2 small garlic cloves, finely minced p. 257

3 chives, minced p. 258

Salt and freshly ground black pepper

1 tablespoon olive oil

Juice of 1 lime p. 203

1   In a small bowl, mash the avocado with a fork. Add the chile, parsley, garlic, chives, and salt and pepper to taste. Switch to a whisk, and as you whisk, very slowly drizzle in the olive oil to help it blend in and lighten the avocado. Whisk in the lime juice, taste, and tweak the seasoning.

2   Use as you would mayonnaise: Spread on sandwiches, toss in chicken or egg salads p. 95, and use for dunking crunchy vegetables. The mayonnaise will taste freshest the day it's made, but thanks to the lime juice, leftovers will stay bright green for about a day in a sealed container in the refrigerator.

THE KEYS TO shockingly easy no-knead focaccia

1) Creamy or foamy = yeast is alive!

2) Stir (don't knead) a shaggy dough, then let it rise in the fridge overnight (or on the counter for 3 to 4 hours)

3) Once it's doubled and bubbly, fold in the edges with two forks to deflate (again, not kneading)

4) Flop into a very well-buttered and oiled pan

5) Once it doubles again, play the piano!

2 snacks for while you wait

Love for the least-popular pepper. And deviled eggs without stuffing deviled eggs.

SERVES 4

2 green bell peppers

1 tablespoon neutral oil, such as canola

Salt

1 teaspoon rice vinegar

½ teaspoon toasted sesame oil

Shichimi togarashi (or red pepper flakes, in a pinch)

Flaky sea salt

SHISHITO-STYLE GREEN PEPPERS
from michele humes

1 With a chef's knife on a cutting board, cut the peppers in half through the stem, pull out the seeds and stem, and slice lengthwise into 1-inch-wide (2.5cm) strips. Heat a wok or large heavy skillet (not nonstick) over high heat. Flick in a drop of water: If it sizzles right away, the pan's hot enough.

2 Swirl in the neutral oil to coat the pan. Add the peppers and a pinch of salt and cook, stirring occasionally with a wooden spoon, until the skin is blistered and the flesh is softening, about 2 minutes. Add the rice vinegar (heads up: it will steam) and sesame oil and cook 30 seconds more, stirring a couple of times. Take the pan off the heat and sprinkle with shichimi togarashi and flaky sea salt to serve.

SERVES 8

¼ teaspoon fine sea salt, plus more for salting the water

4 large eggs

1 celery stalk, peeled

Ice water

½ cup (110g) mayonnaise

1 tablespoon Dijon mustard

1 teaspoon aged red wine vinegar

1 teaspoon hot sauce, plus more for serving

1 teaspoon sliced fresh chives, plus more for serving 🥄 p. 258

½ teaspoon coarsely ground black pepper

4 slices spelt or other multigrain bread, for serving

Lemon wedges, for serving

DEVILED EGG SPREAD
from todd richards

1 In a pot of salty water, boil the eggs for 8 minutes, adding the celery stalk for 2 minutes to soften. Cool both in ice water and peel the eggs 🥄 p. 67. On a cutting board with a chef's knife, cut the eggs in half and pop out the yolks into a medium bowl. Chop the egg whites to equal ½ cup (120ml). (Eat the rest.)

2 Mash the egg yolks with a fork, adding the mayonnaise, Dijon, red wine vinegar, and hot sauce. Finely chop the celery and fold half into the egg yolk mixture. Stir in the chives, pepper, and ¼ teaspoon salt. Toast the bread, smear on the spread, and sprinkle with the remaining celery, chopped egg whites, and chives. Cut each toast into 4 triangles. Serve with lemon and hot sauce. *Soul* author Todd Richards also serves this with canned smoked oysters and smoked trout roe, when you want an even fancier snack.

the quickest pantry dinner short list

TRADITIONAL ROMAN CACIO e pepe needs practice and patience, and vigorous tossing to land a smooth sauce—a technique well worth mastering, though maybe not tonight. But Momofuku Noodle Bar executive chef Tony Kim discovered that miso—the salty Japanese seasoning made from fermented soybeans—will swirl with butter and stock into a remarkably similar cheesy-creamy-fiery sauce with little intervention from you. As Tony wrote in *Lucky Peach* magazine in 2016, "The emulsification process pretty much happens on its own."

Tony also morphed the classic black pepper into a more complex, three-pronged punch of black, white, and tingly Sichuan peppercorns, and replaced the dry Italian pasta with chewy fresh ramen noodles. It's not traditional, but especially on nights it feeds you without acrobatics, you might love it even more.

"cacio" e pepe
from tony kim

SERVES 1, BUT SCALES UP WELL

Salt

1 tablespoon plus 1 teaspoon unsalted butter, softened

2 teaspoons white miso

½ cup (120ml) chicken stock, plus more as needed

1 teaspoon freshly ground Sichuan pepper, plus more for garnish*

1 teaspoon freshly ground white pepper, plus more for garnish*

1 teaspoon freshly ground black pepper, plus more for garnish*

About 5 ounces (140g) fresh ramen noodles (or 3 ounces/85g dry ramen noodles in a pinch)

1 **set up the stove:** Bring a large pot of well-salted water (it should taste very salty, almost like seawater) to a boil over high heat. Meanwhile, in a small bowl, mash together the butter and miso with a fork until smooth. If your butter isn't softened, mash it a couple times to break it into smaller pieces and let it sit near the warm stove till you can blend it smoothly.

2 **melt the miso butter sauce:** In a large saucepan over medium heat, melt the miso butter, then add the chicken stock, Sichuan pepper, white pepper, and black pepper and bring it up to a simmer as you cook your noodles. (If your noodle water isn't boiling yet, turn off the heat under the sauce until it can catch up.)

3 **boil the noodles:** Add the ramen noodles to the boiling pot of water, give them a stir with chopsticks or tongs, and boil until they have just relaxed but are still a littler firmer than you'd like to eat since they will continue cooking in the sauce, 1 to 2 minutes.

4 **get them saucy:** Using chopsticks or tongs, lift the noodles out of the water and into the miso butter sauce. Stir and toss the noodles until the sauce has thickened to lightly coat the noodles and the noodles are still chewy, 1 to 2 minutes more, adding a little more chicken stock or water if the sauce gets too thick. Taste, add a pinch of salt if needed, toss one last time, and pile onto a plate. Sprinkle lightly with a pinch each of the peppers and serve right away.

Great with: Green beans or asparagus blanched in the noodle pot (page 101).

*About Those Peppers
This heat level is perfect for spicy food superfans. If you're not sure, start with half (you can always sprinkle on more). And remember: The finer you grind, the more packed and spicy your teaspoon will be.

Brothy sauce + half-cooked, kind of stiff noodles ↗

A minute or two later . . . thick, glossy sauce + chewy noodles ↘

on blanching (or, how to sneak a side dish into any noodle pot)

an icy plunge

lots of salt in there

hard-core boiling

← towel for draining

Every pot of pasta water can be doing at least two jobs. Because the conditions noodles love—lots of salt, an unruly boil—are exactly what you need to blanch vegetables bright and crisp.

Here's how: Trim tough bits from your vegetables and cut big ones like broccoli or carrots bite-size. Before cooking your pasta, throw them in (in a few batches if you have a lot)—this quick boil kills the enzymes that make vegetables fade.

Then, for a true blanch, scoop the vegetables into an ice bath as soon as they're fork-tender to stop the cooking. If you're feeling lazy or plan to eat them right away, a quick, cold rinse is just fine. Or just throw the veg in partway through cooking the pasta, then drain and eat it all together—an Italian home cooking trick I learned from Mediterranean cooking expert Nancy Harmon Jenkins.

To perk your veg up even more, make extra miso butter (page 98).

How Long Stuff Takes to Blanch, give or Take*

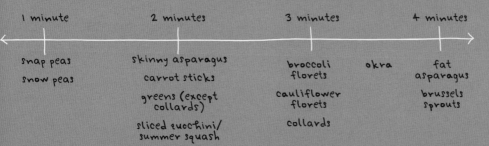

1 minute	2 minutes	3 minutes		4 minutes
snap peas	skinny asparagus	broccoli florets	okra	fat asparagus
snow peas	carrot sticks	cauliflower florets		brussels sprouts
	greens (except collards)	collards		
	sliced zucchini/ summer squash			
	green beans			

*cut in pieces no more than ½ inch (1.3cm) thick (or left whole, if thinner than that)

WHILE EVERY RECIPE in *Indian-ish*, the cookbook by *New York Times* food reporter Priya Krishna and her mom, Ritu, is simple enough that Ritu could cook it after work, this might be the quickest dinner of all.

Ritu and Priya start with masoor dal (especially quick-cooking, split, dehusked pink lentils) and a few well-placed layers of turmeric, salt, lime, and cilantro. But what makes 5 minutes of cooking taste like 5 hours is the joyful hiss of the sizzling spices known as chhonk in Uttar Pradesh, the northern Indian state that Priya's parents immigrated from (and tadka, baghaar, and other regional names elsewhere in India). In seconds, hot ghee—or olive oil, as Ritu and Priya like to use—toasts the spices, which infuse into a crackling spiced oil that jolts the dal to life. While this is a foundational technique in Indian cooking, Priya also uses it in everything from nachos to ramen (page 104).

the most basic dal
from ritu & priya krishna

SERVES 4

DAL

1 cup (190g) masoor dal (aka split and dehusked pink lentils, red lentils, or dhuli masoor)

1 teaspoon ground turmeric

½ teaspoon fine sea salt

3 cups (710ml) water

2 tablespoons lime juice (from about 1 lime) ✤ p. 203

CHHONK

2 teaspoons cumin seeds

2 small dried red chiles

Pinch of ground red chile, such as Kashmiri or cayenne

Pinch of asafetida (optional, but recommended)*

2 tablespoons ghee or olive oil

½ cup (20g) chopped fresh cilantro stems and leaves, for garnish ✤ p. 258

1 **get the dal cooking**: In a large pot over high heat, combine the lentils, turmeric, salt, and water and bring to a boil.

2 **simmer**: Reduce the heat to medium-high, set a long-handled spoon in the pot (this will break the surface tension and keep the lentils from boiling over), and simmer uncovered with the spoon still in the pot until the lentils are soft and slightly mushy, 5 to 7 minutes.

3 **sit**: Take the pot off the heat, cover with a lid or sheet pan, and let sit for 5 minutes. With oven mitts, lift the lid, stir in the lime juice, and set aside.

4 **make the chhonk**: Have the cumin seeds, dried chiles, ground red chile, and asafetida ready by the stove. In a small skillet or pot over medium-high heat, warm the ghee or oil. Once the ghee melts (or the oil starts to shimmer), add the cumin seeds and cook just until they start to sputter and brown, a few seconds. Immediately remove the pan from the heat and stir in the dried chiles, ground red chile, and asafetida.

5 **eat**: Carefully pour the chhonk into the dal (it will sizzle up and feel very exciting), then mix thoroughly. Garnish with the cilantro before serving.

store: Leftovers keep well for a few days in a sealed container in the refrigerator. Warm in the microwave or a small pot over medium heat on the stovetop, stirring and adding a splash of water if it's too thick. Perk up with lime juice and salt if needed.

Great with: Priya suggests rice (page 105) or roti and sliced cucumbers for a superquick, complete meal.

***About That Asafetida**
Priya considers asafetida, or hing in Hindi, the spice that supercharges all others with an irreplaceable oniony funk. Find it online or at Indian grocers, and store it tightly sealed in the pantry.

Make smokier, spicier broiled nachos by pouring over a chhonk made with cumin seeds, paprika, and dried red chiles.

Sizzle an instant chile oil from cumin seeds, star anise, and red pepper flakes for miso ramen or other brothy noodles.

Crackle rosemary and peppercorns in olive oil, then drizzle over a cannellini bean soup 👁️ p. 73.

MICROWAVE RICE (OR QUINOA)

from ritu & priya krishna

Some people depend on their automagic rice cooker every day—but others swear by the microwave for quick, fluffy grains, Priya's family included. A bonus: The bowl is usually easier to clean than a pot and the rice gives your microwave a steam bath as it cooks, too (a perfect time to wipe it down). Rice brands and microwaves vary, so it can take a little trial and error to figure out the right timing, but once you do, you will feel like *you* are the automagic rice cooker.

MAKES 3 CUPS (710ML) COOKED RICE

1 cup (185g) basmati rice*

2 cups (475ml) water

Pinch of salt

1 Set the rice in a fine-mesh strainer, rinse thoroughly under cold running water, and drain. Combine the rice, water, and salt in a medium microwave-safe bowl with a 2-quart (1.9L) capacity (it will need plenty of room to bubble up).

2 Microwave uncovered for 16 to 20 minutes, depending on your microwave. Check on the rice after 8 minutes, and if most of the water is gone, reduce the cooking time. When the rice is done, all the water will have evaporated and there should be grains sticking up on top like grass. Fluff the rice with a fork and let it rest for 10 minutes before serving.

*What About Quinoa?

Priya's family cooks white quinoa—a seed (and complete protein) native to the Andes region in South America that acts like a grain—the same way, adding another ½ cup (120ml) water and cooking for 20 to 23 minutes (checking after 10 minutes, adding more water and time as needed), until the seeds are translucent and their little white tails unfurl.

IN UNDER A MINUTE, these burgers become perilously juicy, with an edge-to-edge salty, beefy crust. Yet they defy one of the most notorious myths of burger-making: *Never smash down your patties or all the juices will escape!* In his *Serious Eats* column The Food Lab, J. Kenji López-Alt untangles the rule, explaining that if you smash your burger *just once*—as soon as it hits the hot skillet, while the meat and fat are still cold—you maximize points of contact with the raging hot pan and Maillard reaction deliciousness (see page 108), but there won't be any juices flowing (yet) to lose.

Kenji knew this technique was the secret weapon of diners and fast-food chains. "But I found myself wondering," he wrote, "what if I were to take this to the extreme?" So he doubled down on the best part— the crispy, flavorful crust—by dividing his patties in two before smashing the dickens out of both.

Maybe best of all, Kenji's ultra-smashed upgrade takes out pretty much all of the guesswork. As long as you have an extremely hot pan and you follow the protocol, this all happens so fast that you don't even need to test anything for doneness, you just need to move (see the whole process go down on page 108).

ultra-smashed cheeseburgers

from j. kenji lópez-alt

SERVES 1 (OR JUST MAKE MORE)

Toppings (think mayonnaise, mustard, shredded lettuce, onions, tomatoes, pickles, or nothing—the burger's that good)

1 soft hamburger bun

4 ounces (110g) good-quality, freshly ground beef chuck

1 tablespoon soft butter

Salt and freshly ground black pepper

1 slice melty cheese, such as American

1 **get ready**: Gather all your toppings. Open your bun, leaving the halves connected if possible, to catch spilling juices. Divide your beef into two 2-ounce (55g) balls, using a digital scale or eyeballing it. Just before cooking your burger, use a table knife to butter and toast the bun (in a toaster oven or under the broiler). Lay your toppings on the bottom bun and have it nearby for when your burger is cooked.

2 **sear one side**: Heat a large cast-iron or stainless steel skillet over high heat for 2 minutes. Set your cold balls of beef in the pan at least 2 inches (5cm) away from each other and the sides of the pan, and immediately smash them down with a stiff metal spatula,* using a second spatula if needed to add pressure (the patties should be about ¼ inch/6mm thick and slightly wider than your average soft burger bun).

3 **flip and eat**: Season the patties generously with a pinch of salt and pepper and let them sear until the bottoms are well-browned and the tops are beginning to turn paler pink and gray in spots, about 45 seconds. Using the back side of the stiff metal spatula, carefully scrape the burger patties up from the pan, making sure to get all of the browned bits. Flip the patties and immediately place a slice of cheese over one patty and stack the second directly on top. Immediately lift the burger stack out of the pan with the spatula and set it on your waiting burger bun. Eat.

Great with: Salty Coke (page 109) and potato chips.

*The Best Smash

If you don't have a good, sturdy spatula for smashing, Food52 commenter Burton D. pre-smashes his patties between layers of wax paper with a rolling pin (a heavy skillet would work, too). You'll still want to press them against the hot pan, but it will take less brute force.

This all happens in about 45 seconds.

1) SMASH

space for steam to escape

hot pan (no oil)

good smasher

2) SCRAPE

ready to flip

back side for scraping leverage

3) FLIP

This is the Maillard reaction (aka when sugars and proteins get hot, mingle, and create delicious browning, named for French biochemist Louis-Camille Maillard and popularized by chemist John E. Hodge) in action!

melt, cheese!

4) STACK

bun in waiting

CHANGE OF ADDRESS (AKA SALTY COKE)
from eric nelson

Make this cheeky cocktail—from Julia Bainbridge's cookbook of booze-free drinks *Good Drinks*—from start to finish if you want to feel like you're tending bar at Eem, a Thai barbecue spot in Portland, Oregon. Or just borrow co-owner Eric Nelson's brilliant idea to season Coke with dashes of soy sauce anytime, especially with a cheeseburger (page 106).

SERVES 2

4 cups (500g) ice cubes

3 tablespoons freshly squeezed lemon juice ☞ p. 203

3 tablespoons maple syrup

2 teaspoons soy sauce

¾ cup (175ml) cold Coca-Cola

Cinnamon stick, to grate for garnish

1   Wrap the ice cubes in a clean kitchen towel, set on a cutting board, and bash with a skillet or rolling pin to make crushed ice. Shake the crushed ice into two tall glasses and keep cold in the freezer (or move quickly on the rest).

2   In a cocktail shaker or Mason jar with a lid, combine the lemon juice, maple syrup, and soy sauce. Fill with more ice cubes, seal the shaker, and shake just to chill and combine, about 3 seconds. Add the Coca-Cola to the shaker, give a quick stir with a long spoon, and pour through a strainer into the glasses filled with crushed ice. Grate cinnamon over the top with a Microplane and serve.

THE COZIEST SOUPS and stews often burble for hours, with noodles cooked separately to avoid turning the broth to sludge. This one is made in 20 minutes and finished with dry pasta slung right into the pot to fend for itself.

You can get away with such shortcuts when you stay tightly focused on a few flavor-driving ingredients, as food stylist Victoria Granof does in her version of this southern Italian staple from her Short Stack edition, *Chickpeas.* She's generous with the olive oil to make up for what would otherwise be an austere soup—don't skimp. As Victoria writes, "It's what'll make you think you're on a balcony in Naples."

In the oil, she toasts smashed garlic till it's browned and nutty. Despite what some cooks might tell you, garlic will only turn bitter if it starts to verge on burnt. Then she fries in tomato paste for frizzled, well-dispersed umami (see page 112). In French culinary school, this technique is called pincé-ing the paste and is used to make hearty brown sauces and stocks. In not-culinary school, it's become my favorite trick for boosting any flat soup or stew: Caramelize a lump of tomato paste in olive oil in a skillet on the side—much like the chhonk on page 102—and unleash it into the pot.

pasta con ceci
from victoria granof

SERVES 2

2 cups (475ml) water

¼ cup (60ml) extra-virgin olive oil, plus more for drizzling

3 garlic cloves, smashed and peeled 👁 p. 257

3 tablespoons tomato paste*

½ teaspoon fine sea salt

1½ cups (250g) drained chickpeas, from 1 (15-ounce/425g) can

½ cup (50g) dry ditalini pasta (or another short shape, like macaroni)

Red pepper flakes, for serving

1 **boil the water and sizzle the base:** In a small pot over high heat, bring the water to a boil. Meanwhile, in a large heavy pot, heat the olive oil over medium heat until it shimmers. Add the garlic and cook, stirring with a wooden spoon, until the garlic is lightly browned and smells a little nutty, about 2 minutes. Stir in the tomato paste and salt and fry until the paste has darkened a shade, about 30 seconds.

2 **simmer the stew:** Carefully add the chickpeas, pasta, and boiling water (it may sizzle and steam at first). Scrape up any browned bits from the bottom of the pot, lower the heat, and simmer, stirring occasionally, until the pasta is tender and as brothy or stewy as you like, 15 to 20 minutes. Taste and tweak the salt as needed.

3 **eat:** To serve, ladle the pasta into shallow bowls, sprinkle with red pepper flakes, and drizzle a bit of olive oil on top.

Great with: A feisty green salad (page 113).

*What About the Rest of the Can?
Dollop extra tomato paste by the tablespoon onto a plate and stick it in the freezer, then store the little tomato snowballs in a freezer-safe container for any recipe. Or buy the kind in a tube, which keeps almost forever in the fridge.

Toasty garlic, check. Caramelized tomato paste, check.

Dry pasta soaks up flavor and thickens the stew
(and boiling water helps it cook fast)

SALAD OF GRAND RAPIDS LETTUCE LEAVES & ROMAINE
from edna lewis

In this elegant salad from her cookbook *The Taste of Country Cooking*, the late icon of seasonal American cooking Edna Lewis taught us that while oil is good in vinaigrettes, it's by no means necessary if you let a little sugar and time soften the vinegar. Without oil, there's no need to rush to eat the salad before it wilts. Miss Lewis, as she was known to many, used Grand Rapids lettuce grown on her farm, along with romaine, but any crunchy lettuces work well.

1 In a Mason jar or small bowl, combine the vinegar, sugar, salt, and pepper. Shake the dressing, or stir with a wooden spoon, until all the salt has dissolved. Add the lettuce and scallions to a serving bowl.

2 Pour the dressing over the lettuce and scallions and set aside until the rest of the meal is ready. The dressing will mellow nicely as it sits, and the salad will hold for an hour without wilting, since it has no oil.

SERVES 4 TO 5

¼ cup (60ml) vinegar*

2 teaspoons sugar

¼ teaspoon fine sea salt

⅛ teaspoon freshly ground black pepper

4 cups (110g) crisp lettuce leaves, torn in bite-size pieces

4 or 5 scallions, sliced thin with some green top added p. 137

*About That Vinegar
In *The Taste of Country Cooking*, Edna Lewis left the type of vinegar up to the cook but used white and cider vinegars in other recipes. Try either one and decide what you like.

THIS RECIPE PROVES that homemade soup can be simple and swift by doing away with the decision that most often gets in the way: Do I buy a carton of stock that just doesn't taste all that good? Or take the time to make a homemade broth from scraps and bones (page 81)? This soup says: You'll be fine doing neither.

In her cookbook *Vietnamese Food Any Day*, Andrea Nguyen shared this recipe for canh, the simple brothy soup her mom made five nights a week, as many Vietnamese families do. It quickly creates its own flavorful broth as the water vigorously boils with softened onions and a good dose of fish sauce, then greens, ginger, and a protein join in to round out the flavor. Plunk in quick-cooking fish or shrimp, leftover roasted chicken (page 76), or Andrea's Soy-Seared Tofu (page 117)—my longtime favorite way to cook tofu by heart.

canh

from andrea nguyen

SERVES 4

Soy-Seared Tofu 👜 p. 117, 12 large peeled and deveined shrimp, or 6 ounces (170g) white fish like rockfish or bass

1 tablespoon neutral oil, such as canola

½ medium yellow or red onion, thinly sliced 👜 p. 256

5½ cups (1.3L) water

½ teaspoon fine sea salt

1 tablespoon fish sauce, plus more as needed

1 (8-ounce/225g) bunch mustard greens, coarsely chopped, including tender stems 👜 p. 48

1½ teaspoons finely chopped peeled ginger 👜 p. 260

Freshly ground black pepper (optional)

1   **prep the protein:** Make the tofu or, on a cutting board with a paring knife, split the shrimp in half lengthwise or cut the fish into bite-size chunks.

2   **make the broth:** In a 3- or 4-quart (2.8 or 3.8L) pot over medium heat, warm the oil. When the oil is starting to shimmer, add the onion and cook, stirring with a wooden spoon, until soft and sweet-smelling, about 4 minutes. Add the water, salt, and fish sauce, then raise the heat to medium-high and bring to a boil. Boil vigorously for 3 to 5 minutes to develop the broth's flavor.

3   **add the greens, ginger, and protein:** Add the greens, stirring occasionally to help them cook evenly. When the greens are very soft, about 5 minutes, add the ginger and shrimp, fish, or tofu and continue simmering just until the protein is opaque 👜 p. 129, p. 155, 1 to 2 minutes (if you're using tofu, don't worry about simmering more— it's already cooked!). Turn off the heat, slide the pot to a cool burner, and let it rest for 5 to 10 minutes, uncovered.

4   **eat:** Taste and add additional salt or fish sauce, if needed. Ladle the soup into individual serving bowls and sprinkle with pepper, if you like. Eat immediately.

store: The soup will keep in a sealed container in the refrigerator for 5 days. Warm up in the microwave or in a pot on the stovetop over medium-high heat.

Great with: Warm bread and butter or rice (page 105) and crunchy veggies with coconut water nuoc cham (page 165).

1) Tofu absorbs soy sauce like a sponge . . .

2) . . . then gets dry enough to sear in the oil (wet things don't brown well)

3) Onions + water + fish sauce = speedy stock . . .

4) . . . + greens + ginger = soup!

SOY-SEARED TOFU

from andrea nguyen

Andrea developed this counterintuitive technique to skip having to press or freeze tofu in advance to squeeze out extra moisture. Instead, the liquid evaporates in the dry nonstick pan, leaving the tofu no choice but to drink up soy sauce, then sear in sizzling oil—in that order.

SERVES 2 TO 4

1 (14-ounce/400g) block extra-firm tofu

1 tablespoon soy sauce*

1 tablespoon neutral oil, such as canola

*About That Soy Sauce
If you only have low-sodium soy sauce, season with a little extra salt to taste.

1   Drain the tofu and pat it dry with a clean kitchen towel. On a cutting board with a chef's knife, slice the tofu crosswise into two pieces, then slice each piece crosswise into four pieces, for a total of eight rectangles (they should look like big dominoes). Lay them in a large nonstick skillet in a single layer. Drizzle over the soy sauce and flip to coat both sides.

2   Cook over medium heat until nicely browned and dry on the bottom, about 5 minutes. Drizzle the oil over the tofu, then use a wide (not metal) spatula to flip them. If the tofu is sticking, patiently fry a little longer. If it doesn't easily flip, use the back side of the spatula to scrape up as much of the browned surface as you can before flipping.

3   Let cook long enough to brown the second side, 4 to 5 minutes. Shake the skillet to see if the tofu will dislodge from the bottom. When there is a little movement, flip the tofu over to add extra color to the first side, if needed. When both sides are a rich, mottled brown with dark brown edges, lift the tofu onto a cooling rack (optional) to dry for about 5 minutes before serving (or add directly to the soup on page 114).

4   The tofu will keep in a sealed container in the refrigerator for 5 days. Eat at room temperature or gently reheat in a nonstick skillet over medium heat with a little oil.

2 swift pasta sauces

A spicy number that proves lemon zest makes tomatoes taste brighter and juicier. And 10-minute noodles, cooked right in their own buttery sauce.

SERVES 8

¼ cup (60ml) extra-virgin olive oil

1½ teaspoons red pepper flakes, or to taste

½ teaspoon fine sea salt

3 medium garlic cloves, finely chopped 👑 p. 257

1 (28-ounce/794g) can crushed red tomatoes with no added herbs or seasonings (basil is okay)

Zest of 1 lemon 👑 p. 203

FIVE-MINUTE TOMATO SAUCE
from heidi swanson

1   In a cold saucepan, combine the olive oil, red pepper flakes, salt, and garlic, then set over medium-high heat. Stir with a wooden spoon as it heats and, once it starts to sizzle, cook just until everything is fragrant without browning the garlic, 45 seconds or so.

2   Stir in the tomatoes and heat to a gentle simmer, about 2 minutes. Remove from the heat, carefully taste, and add salt as needed.

3   Stir in most of the lemon zest, saving a bit to sprinkle. Serve with any pasta you like.

SERVES 1

2 tablespoons
unsalted butter

2 ounces (55g) angel hair
pasta

1 cup (240ml) hot chicken
stock, heated in the
microwave or on the stove

Freshly ground
black pepper

½ lemon

Salt, if needed

LEMON-BUTTER ANGEL HAIR
from sue kreitzman

1 In a small pot with a lid nearby, melt the butter over medium heat. With your hands,
   break up the pasta into bite-size lengths, 1 to 2 inches (2.5 to 5cm) each, and add them
   to the pot. With a wooden spoon, toss the pasta in the butter until it is well-coated.

2 Pour in the hot stock and grind in a few turns of pepper. Turn the heat down to low, cover
   the pot, and cook until all the liquid is absorbed, about 10 minutes.

3 Squeeze in some lemon juice. Stir, taste, and adjust the lemon, salt, and pepper. Serve hot.

more good (active) weeknight dinners you can make in under an hour

THE PAD THAI sauce that chef Kris Yenbamroong makes at his Night + Market restaurants in Los Angeles is the same one you can make with ingredients from virtually any supermarket. This isn't convenience for convenience's sake: It's because this is the way Kris's grandma Vilai—the original chef at his family's restaurant Talesai—has always made it and how he wants it to taste.

"I like my sauce to be direct and sharp, which is why I use white sugar and white vinegar as opposed to the subtler (and harder to find) palm sugar and tamarind water," Kris writes in his *Night + Market* cookbook. Since the recipe is done in all of 3 minutes (once your noodles have soaked for 30 minutes), it can take a few tries to move quickly and confidently, but there are photos of every step on pages 124–125, and all practice runs will be delicious—and *fast*.

pad thai

from kris yenbamroong

SERVES 1 TO 2

4 ounces (115g) dried rice stick noodles (⅛ to ⅓ inch/ 3 to 8mm wide)

2 tablespoons sugar

2 tablespoons fish sauce

2 tablespoons distilled white vinegar

3 tablespoons neutral oil, such as canola

4 ounces (115g) extra-firm or pressed tofu, cut into bite-size slices (or large peeled shrimp)

1 large egg

1 cup (50g) bean sprouts*

2 scallions, cut very thinly on an angle into 2-inch-long (5cm) slices
👁 p. 137

1 lime wedge

2 tablespoons crushed roasted peanuts

1 teaspoon roasted chile powder*

1 **30 minutes before dinner, get ready:** Soak the noodles in a pan of warm water for 30 minutes, until they'll bend around your finger, then drain in a colander. In a small bowl with a spoon, stir together the sugar, fish sauce, and vinegar to make the sauce. Gather your ingredients near the stove—the cooking moves fast.

2 **stir-fry the protein:** Heat an empty wok or large skillet (not nonstick) over high heat until it begins to smoke, then swirl in the oil to coat the pan. Add the tofu and cook, stirring with a spatula until it turns golden brown, about 1 minute (if using shrimp, cook until they start to turn pink but aren't fully cooked, 30 seconds or less).

3 **add the noodles and sauce:** Add the drained noodles, pour in the sauce, and cook, stirring constantly, until the noodles absorb the sauce, about 1 minute.

4 **scramble in the egg:** Use your spatula to make an empty space in the center of the wok. Crack the egg into the space and let it cook until the edges start to set, 15 to 20 seconds. Break up and scramble the egg with the spatula, scraping the bottom of the wok. When the egg is still soft, toss it back in with the noodles. Once the egg looks mostly firm and cooked, move the wok to a cool burner.

5 **eat:** Stir in the bean sprouts and scallions. Serve on a plate (or two) and garnish with a lime wedge and small piles of peanuts and chile powder for sprinkling as you eat.

make ahead and store: Soak the noodles ahead, then drain and keep in a container in the fridge. Pad Thai is best fresh, but leftovers will keep in a sealed container in the fridge for a couple of days and reheat in the microwave or a skillet over medium heat, stirring often and adding a splash of water if they get too dry.

Great with: A cold beer or seltzer with lime.

*A Couple of Helpful Backups
If you can't find fresh bean sprouts, thinly sliced celery or cabbage are good, crunchy substitutes. Roasted chile powder—made from sun-dried Thai bird chiles—is fruity, complex, and worth picking up at an Asian grocery store or online, but you can use other ground chiles in a pinch.

1) Soak your noodles till they can do this

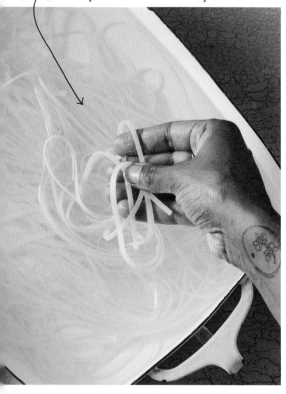

2) Cook tofu till it's golden (or shrimp till it's turning pink)

3) Stir in the soaked noodles and sauce, just till the sauce is absorbed

5) ... before
stirring through

4) Scramble the egg
roughly on its own ...

6) Throw in crunchy bits (off the heat)

LOUISIANA BARBECUED SHRIMP is that sort of magical dish that's intensely flavorful, quick to cook, and perfect for sharing—all you need to do is spend a few minutes revving at the spice drawer first. Despite the name, the recipe isn't cooked on a barbecue but simmered straight in a spicy-bright pan sauce. As Toni Tipton-Martin explains in her book *Jubilee*, drawn from her collection of nearly 400 African American cookbooks, "'Barbecue shrimp' is just the name Louisiana Creole cooks assigned to shrimp braised in wine, beer, or a garlic butter sauce." This one is Toni's favorite version, based on one from the late model/chef/restaurateur B. Smith.

Sometimes, Toni doesn't even wait to get the shrimp out of the pan, serving it in the kitchen as an appetizer, right in the skillet it's cooked in, with lots of hot crusty bread to get every bit of sauce. No more than 10 minutes have passed.

louisiana barbecued shrimp

from toni tipton-martin

SERVES 2 TO 4

½ teaspoon cayenne

½ teaspoon dried thyme

½ teaspoon dried oregano

¼ teaspoon fine sea salt

¼ teaspoon black pepper

¼ teaspoon red pepper flakes

¼ teaspoon paprika

2 dried bay leaves, broken into large pieces

¼ cup (60g) unsalted butter

2 garlic cloves, minced
p. 257

¼ cup (60ml) white wine

½ cup (120ml) fish or chicken stock

2 tablespoons freshly squeezed lemon juice
p. 203

2 tablespoons Worcestershire sauce

1 pound (450g) shell-on shrimp p. 129

2 tablespoons minced fresh parsley p. 258

Hot crusty French bread, for serving*

1 **get prepped**: In a small bowl, combine the cayenne, thyme, oregano, salt, black pepper, red pepper flakes, paprika, and bay leaves. Gather the rest of your ingredients near the stove.

2 **make the sauce**: In a large cast-iron skillet over medium-high heat, melt the butter until sizzling. Add the garlic, spices, wine, stock, lemon juice, and Worcestershire sauce. Bring to a boil, then reduce the heat and simmer until the sauce is thick enough to lightly coat a spoon (if you dip the spoon in the sauce, let it cool briefly, then swipe your finger across the back of the spoon; it should leave a trail p. 128), 5 to 7 minutes. Instead of stirring, shake the pan gently as it cooks to help bring the sauce together.

3 **simmer the shrimp**: Add the shrimp, reduce the heat to low, and cook until the shrimp turn pink and firm p. 129, turning once with tongs or a spatula, 3 to 5 minutes.

4 **eat**: Sprinkle the shrimp with parsley and serve immediately in shallow bowls or directly from the skillet with hot French bread to swipe up the sauce. Peel the shrimp with your hands and eat. (Pros would recommend sucking the sauce off the shrimp before peeling.)

Great with: A cold beer or iced tea.

*Ready Your Bread
To have your bread good and hot when your shrimp are done, heat the oven to 300°F (150°C) before you start cooking, then pop in your loaf on a sheet pan for 5 to 10 minutes. If it's a little stale, quickly wet just the crust under running water first.

red pepper flakes

black pepper

dried oregano

paprika

bay leaves

dried thyme →

cayenne

1) This is how you spark big flavor in a 5-minute sauce

2) Shake the sauce to bring it together . . .

3) . . . till it coats a spoon enough to leave a t
with your finger—then send in the shrimp

Is My Shrimp Done?

Shrimp is such a supportive little protein that not only does it cook in moments, but as soon as it turns from gray to pink, you know it's done.

A note on buying shrimp: Like all seafood and other animal-based proteins, the type of shrimp you choose to buy can make a big impact on the environment and the local community that sources them—all good reasons to pay a little more for shrimp that have been harvested responsibly and to eat and appreciate them in moderation. As a bonus, they'll taste a lot better, too. Guides such as Monterey Bay Aquarium's Seafood Watch, or a fishmonger who likes talking about where their seafood comes from, can help.

NOPE

Squishy, gray, raw

ALMOST THERE

Getting firmer and pinker,
but a little gray squish

YES!

Firm, pink, pull it!

TOO FAR, BUT WILL BE OKAY

A little drier and chewier, but
a really good sauce cures all

THIS RECIPE IS the cure-all for one of our more maddening experiences as home cooks: seeing good food go to waste. Half-bunches of fresh herbs, wilting arugula, and the floppy green tops from radishes, turnips, and beets are the worst offenders—we don't always know what to do with them, and they turn on us fast.

In her Food52 series *Off-Script with Sohla*, chef Sohla El-Waylly handed us a formula for quickly morphing any lost herbs and greens into a deeply flavored bowl of beans, greens, umami, and comfort. Here are the keys so you can go off-script, too.

Speed up your pasta cooking by soaking it in flavorful liquids or even just water while you cook everything else—a trick borrowed from Sohla's friends at Ideas in Food (see page 55). Jump-start a stew with lots of anchovies and garlic and you can use water instead of stock (and not miss it). Swirl in yogurt and butter at the very end, off the heat, to pad any bitterness or other sharp edges. And brighten with lemon, always. You'll start asking farmers for their extra beet greens, just to make more.

tiny pasta with tender herbs, chickpeas & yogurt
from sohla el waylly

SERVES 2 TO 4

1½ cups (150g) dry ditalini pasta (or another short shape, like macaroni)

3 cups (710ml) chicken or vegetable stock or water, divided

3 tablespoons butter, divided

3 anchovy fillets

3 garlic cloves, chopped
👆 p. 257

6 cups (140g) roughly chopped tender herbs and/or greens (like dill, parsley, basil, arugula, radish tops, and beet tops), plus a handful for garnish 👆 p. 258

Salt and freshly ground black pepper

1½ cups (250g) drained chickpeas, from 1 (15-ounce/425g) can

⅓ cup (80ml) whole-milk Greek yogurt, plus more for serving

Lemon zest and juice, to taste 👆 p. 203

1 **soak the pasta**: Put the pasta in a small bowl and cover with 1½ cups (355ml) of the stock or water. Stir occasionally with a wooden spoon to make sure the pasta isn't clumping together.

2 **sizzle the aromatics**: Heat a medium Dutch oven or other pot with a lid nearby over medium heat, add 2 tablespoons of the butter, and melt until foamy, about 2 minutes. Add the anchovies and garlic and cook, stirring often, until the anchovies melt into the fat and the garlic just begins to brown and smells delicious, 3 to 5 minutes.

3 **braise the greens and chickpeas**: Add the herbs and/or greens, the remaining 1½ cups (355ml) stock or water, a pinch of salt, and a few grinds of pepper. Turn up the heat to high and bring to a boil, then reduce the heat to a steady simmer. Add the chickpeas and cook, partially covered with the lid, until the greens are tender and silky and the liquid has reduced to about 1 cup (240ml), 10 to 15 minutes. Taste the greens and add more salt and pepper if needed. You want it to be very delicious and well-seasoned at this point to help flavor the pasta.

4 **add the pasta**: Add the pasta along with the soaking liquid and simmer, stirring frequently, until the pasta is al dente (cool and taste a noodle—it should be tender, with a little resistance, and taste great, 3 to 5 minutes). If you want it brothier, splash in a little more stock or water. Turn off the heat and, with oven mitts, slide the pot to a cool burner and stir in the yogurt and the remaining 1 tablespoon butter. Season with Microplaned lemon zest and a squeeze of lemon juice to taste and add more salt and pepper if needed.

continued

tiny pasta with tender herbs, chickpeas & yogurt
continued

5 **eat**: Ladle the pasta into bowls and garnish with more yogurt and fresh herbs if you like.

store: Leftovers keep well in a sealed container in the fridge for a few days. The pasta will keep absorbing liquid as it sits, so you may need to add more stock or water when you reheat—either in the microwave or in a pot on medium heat on the stovetop, stirring. Tweak the seasoning and brighten with more lemon juice if you like.

Great with: Crunchy salad (page 113) and soft focaccia (page 88).

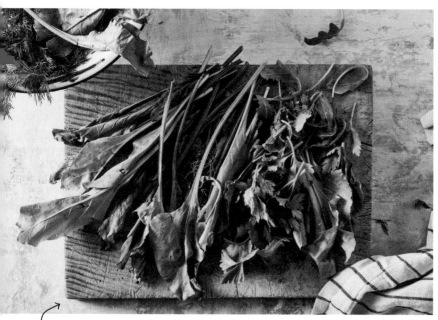

All tender tops, herbs, and slumping salad greens welcome here

Soaked pasta is quicker-cooking and you bonus starchy (i.e., thickening) we

HOW TO
trick herbs into staying fresh

If you toss fragile herbs in a crisper drawer still bundled in bags from the store, you'll be lucky if they last a few days. I'm always shocked by how much longer they stay perky—sometimes by weeks—when I take a couple of minutes to set them up like cut flowers from the get-go.

1) Trim the bottoms so they can drink up water, toss any twist ties, then rinse and dry them well (page 185)

2) Ditch any wilted sprigs and stand them up in a jar with an inch (2.5cm) of water

3a) Drape a plastic bag over to trap humidity and seal it up

3b) Or use J. Kenji López-Alt's no-spill alternative: a sealed quart-size (950ml) Mason jar or deli container

4) Keep in the fridge (except basil—it really prefers to stay uncovered on the counter). If the water gets murky, replace it with fresh

A FEW ALTERNATIVES:

- Palatial fridge? Store herbs washed and spun in the salad spinner.

- No room? Wrap in a damp towel in a produce bag and plan on using them quicker.

- Once your herbs are looking wilted (but not yellow or slimy—those are compost), you can sometimes revive them by soaking in cold water for a few minutes, or just wilt them into soups and stews (page 130).

OF ALL THE techniques taught in culinary schools and beginner cookbooks, the one that irks me the most is the tomato concassé, in which you remove the skin, seeds, and juice—and along with them, much of the flavor, texture, and joy—of the tomato.

I'm much happier following Leah Chase, the late chef of Dooky Chase's Restaurant in New Orleans for seven decades. In her cookbook *And Still I Cook*, she called for chopped ripe tomatoes, emphatically *with seeds*, as the base for a swift, vibrant sauce. It would brighten anything from fried eggs (page 14) to creamy polenta (page 175) to slow-roasted salmon (page 152), but in this recipe, the Queen of Creole Cuisine spooned the sauce onto pancakes plumped up with leftover rice from the fridge. The extra heft makes pancakes that feel like a full meal, and none of it lacks in joy.

rice pancakes with ham & tomato-basil sauce
from leah chase

SERVES 4

RICE PANCAKES

2 large eggs

2 cups (320g) cooked rice
🍲 p. 105

½ cup (60g) self-rising flour*

1½ teaspoons fine sea salt

½ teaspoon white pepper

½ cup (120ml) milk, preferably whole

¼ cup (60ml) neutral oil, such as canola

HAM & TOMATO-BASIL SAUCE

1 tablespoon unsalted butter

8 ounces (225g) thickly sliced ham, chopped (about 1½ cups)

2 cups (360g) chopped ripe fresh tomatoes, with seeds

4 scallions, sliced 🍲 p. 137

2 fresh jalapeño chiles, seeded and chopped
🍲 p. 70

1 teaspoon chopped basil
🍲 p. 258

½ teaspoon garlic salt

1 **make the rice pancake batter:** In a small bowl, crack the eggs, then beat well with a fork. In a medium bowl, combine the rice, flour, salt, and pepper and stir well with a wooden spoon. Slowly pour in the eggs while continuing to stir, then add the milk and beat everything together well.

2 **cook the pancakes:** Set a large heavy skillet over medium-high heat and pour in the oil. When the oil is hot enough that a drop of batter sizzles right away, use a large spoon or ¼-cup (60ml) measuring cup to scoop the batter into the pan, leaving about 3 inches (7.5cm) between each pancake. Cook until golden on one side, about 4 minutes, then use a wide spatula to flip each one and brown the other side, about 4 minutes. With the spatula, lift the pancakes to a platter.

3 **make the sauce and eat:** Carefully wipe out the skillet with a kitchen towel or paper towel, then set over medium-low heat to melt the butter. Add the ham and stir to coat. Turn up the heat to medium, add the tomatoes, scallions, and peppers, and sauté until softened, about 5 minutes. Lower the heat to medium-low, add the basil and garlic salt, and cook until saucy and fragrant, 5 minutes more. Serve spooned over the rice pancakes.

store: Leftover pancakes and sauce will keep well in separate sealed containers in the refrigerator for a few days. To crisp the pancakes, heat on a sheet pan under the broiler, flipping once (watch closely so they don't burn). Heat the sauce in the microwave or in a small pot over medium heat on the stovetop, stirring occasionally.

Great with: Corn on the cob, warmed in a pot of just-boiled water for a few minutes.

*No Self-Rising Flour?
If you don't have self-rising flour, you can swap in ½ cup (60g) all-purpose flour, ¾ teaspoon baking powder, and 1¼ teaspoons fine sea salt.

Leftover rice's new starring role: turning pancakes into dinner

In this joyful sauce, tomato skins, juice, and seeds are all welcome

cleaning, cutting & cloning scallions

Scallions may be more approachable than their other introverted allium cousins like onions (see page 256) and shallots (see page 207), but there are still a few helpful tricks for getting the most out of them—and even more bunches of scallions, grown right on your windowsill.

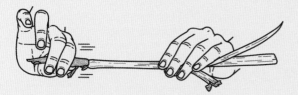

1) Pull off any scraggly, dirty bits and give the scallions a rinse

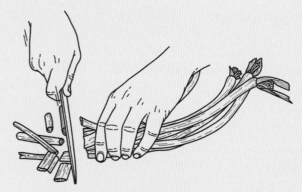

2) Line them up on a cutting board to trim any bruised tops

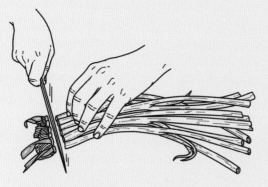

3) Trim just the hairy root, leaving the bulb mostly intact. Unless...

4) . . . you want to regrow your scallions. Save the bottom inch (2.5 cm) with the root, prop up in a clear glass with a little water, set in the sunlight, and trim and eat the greens that shoot up (change the water when it's murky)

A few scallion-slicing options:

rounds

bias

super extreme bias

matchsticks

RISOTTO HAS A reputation for being needy: Needing one pot for simmering stock and another for the rice to plump up and make its own silky sauce. Needing to be continuously ladled and stirred, ladled and stirred. The whole act can be meditative and even fun—in a witch-standing-over-a-bubbling-cauldron sort of way—but, as it turns out, all that effort is *not* strictly needed.

As Judy Rodgers, the late chef and driving force behind San Francisco's Zuni Café, wrote in *The Zuni Café Cookbook*, "I started experimenting with cold, warm, and hot stock and found I could make a creamy risotto with any one." She also wasn't concerned about how often you add more stock, as long as the grains don't dry out. "It is only the final doses that require thoughtful judgment, to make sure you don't add more stock than an al dente grain needs."

This means you can grab any stock out of your fridge or pantry to start your risotto—and roam the kitchen making salad and putting away dishes as it cooks, no longer tethered to the pot. "This convenient heresy alarms even longtime cooks at Zuni," she continued, "but it has not failed me." In this citrus version, Judy stirred in chunks of fresh grapefruit and lime that dissolve into colorful flecks, but you can use her convenient heresy with any mix-ins you like.

one-pot citrus risotto
from judy rodgers

SERVES 4 TO 6

2 tablespoons unsalted butter

½ cup (55g) finely chopped yellow onion 🍵 p. 256

Salt

2 cups (360g) Carnaroli or Arborio rice

4 to 5 cups (950ml to 1.2L) chicken stock, divided*

¾ cup (165g) grapefruit segments plus juice, from 1 to 2 medium grapefruit 🍵 p. 142

A scant ¼ cup (50g) lime segments, from 1 lime 🍵 p. 142

¼ cup (60ml) mascarpone

1 **sauté the onion:** In a 4-quart (3.8L) saucepan or another medium pot over medium-low heat, melt the butter. Add the onion and a few pinches of salt and cook, stirring regularly with a wooden spoon, until the onion is tender and translucent, about 6 minutes.

2 **simmer the rice:** Add the rice and stir until the grains are warm and glossy. Pour in about 2 cups (475ml) of the stock, adjusting the heat to let it gently simmer, then stir occasionally until it has been mostly absorbed. Add another cup (240ml) or so of stock and repeat. The risotto should be starting to look like a porridge. Taste and adjust the seasoning—the rice will still be hard and a little raw tasting. Add another ½ cup (120ml) or so of stock and stir as needed until just absorbed. Taste and adjust the seasoning again.

3 **stir in the citrus:** Break the citrus sections into irregular chunks as you add them to the risotto. Add the grapefruit juice—if your grapefruit was very juicy, you may not need much of the remaining stock.

continued

*Stock Matters
Use stock that's likely to taste fresh and delicious, like homemade (page 81) or one sold at a butcher or in the freezer section. Judy preferred plain water to a flat-tasting boxed broth. I've also made superquick stocks alongside my risotto pot, by heating up water with mashed overripe tomatoes, smashed garlic cloves, herbs, anchovies, or Parmesan rinds.

one-pot citrus risotto

continued

4 **beat in the mascarpone and eat**: Taste again: If the rice is still quite firm, add more stock, a tablespoon at a time, and cook until the rice is still just a little firm in the center (al dente). Turn off the heat and aggressively stir in the mascarpone until the risotto is creamy and the citrus is broken down into pretty flecks. Serve immediately.

make ahead and store: The segments and juice can be made the day before (and onion chopped, too) and kept in sealed containers in the fridge. Leftover risotto will firm up in the fridge and won't be as creamy but can be turned into other delicious things p. 143.

Great with: Slow-roasted salmon (page 152) and snap peas seared in a skillet with olive oil.

2) When the rice is just a tad too hard in the center, add the citrus

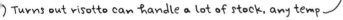

) Turns out risotto can handle a lot of stock, any temp

3) When the rice is al dente and delicious, beat in the mascarpone to make it creamy and polka-dotted

slice & segment citrus

When you want lemons, limes, grapefruits, oranges, or other round citrus freed of skin and ready to eat in anything from yogurt (page 22) to salad (page 231) to risotto (page 138), your best tool is a paring knife.

You can simply cut the fruit into pretty wheels—or go all the way and segment it, to whittle away even the thin membrane that neatly bundles each section.

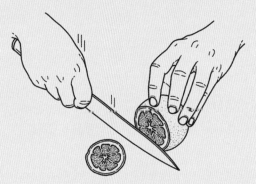

1) Slice off about ½ inch (1.3cm) from both ends

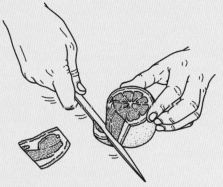

2) Carve away all the skin and white pith, curving from top to bottom

TO SLICE:

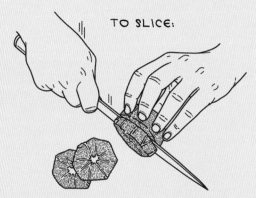

1) Slice crosswise into pretty wheels—easy!

TO SEGMENT:

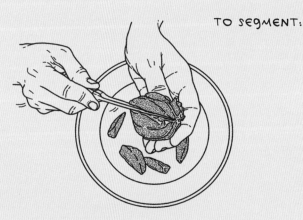

1) Over a bowl, slide the knife along each white membrane to free all the wedge-shaped segments

2) Squeeze the last juice from the leftover membrane—less easy but fun!

RISOTTO AL SALTO

from rose gray & ruth rogers

Salto means "jump" in Italian (much like the French word "sauté"), and many recipes do call for flipping this cake made from leftover risotto to crisp both sides. This one, adapted from *The River Café Cookbook* by Ruth Rogers and the late Rose Gray, leaves the underside creamy and requires much less precision.

SERVES 1 PERSON PER CUP OF LEFTOVER RISOTTO

Butter (1 tablespoon per cup of leftover risotto)

Leftover risotto 👁 p.138

Parmesan, for serving

1   Melt the butter over medium heat in a large nonstick skillet and swirl to coat the pan. With a wide (not metal) spatula, press the cool risotto into the pan to about 1 inch (2.5cm) thick. Fry until crisp and browned (you'll see browning at the edges and can lift a side slightly with the spatula to peek), about 5 minutes.

2   Turn off the heat and slide the skillet off the burner. With the spatula, loosen the cake to make sure it isn't sticking and can slide around in the pan with gentle shaking. Grab two large flat plates. Gently slide the cake out onto one plate, crisp-side down, then top the cake with the second, upside-down plate. With oven mitts, hold the stack of plates with both hands and carefully flip over, then remove the top plate. Cut in wedges with a table knife and serve topped with Parmesan freshly grated with a Microplane.

LASAGNA IS THE dinner everyone wants, but no one thinks they have time to make. But in this one-skillet recipe from Kathy Brennan and Caroline Campion's cookbook, *Keepers*, you do every step right in the pan, from browning the sausage, to mashing up the canned tomatoes, to poking in the noodles, to simmering it all into a saucy, cheesy mass, all within 45 minutes. (Or skip the sausage and make it vegetarian, throwing in a teaspoon of fennel seeds to mimic the flavor, a tip from Food52 reader Cheryl D.)

This all-access technique also gives you chances to interact and taste as you cook to ensure lasagna success, and just enough time to wash dishes and throw together a side (see page 148). I've tried other skillet lasagna recipes, but they've ended up more like pasta stews or required just as much work and dirty dishes as their longer-cooked counterparts. This is the one that stuck. It's a keeper.

skillet lasagna
from kathy brennan & caroline campion

SERVES 6

1 pound (450g) sweet or hot Italian sausages

2 tablespoons olive oil

1 small yellow onion, finely chopped ☞ p. 256

4 garlic cloves, minced ☞ p. 257

Large pinch of red pepper flakes

1 teaspoon dried oregano

1 sprig basil, plus a handful of basil leaves

2 (28-ounce/794g) cans whole, peeled tomatoes

Salt and freshly ground black pepper

1 (9-ounce/255g) package no-boil lasagna noodles*

4 ounces (115g) mascarpone cheese or cream cheese (½ cup)

8 ounces (225g) fresh mozzarella, thinly sliced and patted dry

1 **brown the sausage:** Set the sausages on a plate, slit each casing open with a paring knife, peel it away from the meat, and discard. In a large high-sided sauté pan or Dutch oven with a 3-quart (2.8L) capacity, heat the oil over high heat until it shimmers. Add the sausages and cook, stirring with a wooden spoon and breaking up the meat, until browned, about 4 minutes. Turn down the heat to medium-low and, leaving as much oil behind in the pan as you can, scoop the sausage into a medium bowl and set aside.

2 **make the sauce:** Add the onion, garlic, and red pepper flakes to the pan and cook, stirring occasionally, until the onion is softened, about 7 minutes. Add the oregano, the sprig of basil, and the tomatoes and their juices, crushing the tomatoes as you add them with your hands or a potato masher (consider wearing an apron or dark shirt—the tomatoes will squirt).

3 Add the cooked sausage and any juices. Season with a pinch of salt and a few grinds of pepper, then gently simmer for 5 minutes, stirring occasionally. (Canned tomatoes can vary—if the sauce is really soupy, let the liquid boil off until it's thick and saucy; if it looks dry, add a little water.) Taste and adjust the seasoning (it should be a little salty) and pull out the basil sprig.

continued

*About Those Noodles
No-boil noodle packages aren't all this size, so be sure to check. You can also use regular lasagna noodles or even other shapes—they'll likely take a bit longer to cook and you may need to add more water.

4 **add the noodles**: Break half of the lasagna noodles in half crosswise (don't worry if smaller pieces break off—they'll go in, too) and, as you do so, push each piece into the sauce under the sausage, distributing them evenly around the pan (it can help to do this off the heat, and to use an extra noodle to nudge them under—try to leave a little cushion of sauce beneath them, so they don't stick to the bottom and burn).

5 Break the rest of the noodles in half and distribute them evenly on top of the sauce, then push down on them with the back of your spoon to submerge them. Cover the pan with a lid or sheet pan and gently simmer, raising the heat a little, if needed, until the noodles are tender and the sauce has thickened slightly, about 12 minutes. (Use oven mitts to lift the lid and peek.)

6 **top, melt, and eat**: Spoon the mascarpone on top of the lasagna and swirl it into the sauce. Scatter the mozzarella on top, cover, and gently simmer until the cheese is melted, about 2 minutes. Take the pan off the heat and top with the fresh basil leaves, tearing any large ones. Let the lasagna sit, uncovered, for about 10 minutes, then serve.

make ahead and store: Lasagna can be made the day before, left to cool slightly before storing tightly sealed in the fridge, and reheated in a 350°F (175°C) oven. Leftovers keep well covered in the fridge for 5 days (or in the freezer for 3 months) and can be microwaved or warmed in the oven.

Great with: Lemony fennel salad (page 148) and gelato (page 244) for dessert.

1) Squish canned tomatoes in with your hands ⤵
   (look out for squirting juice)

3) Top with swirly mascarpone and
   mozzarella, then melt under a lid

2) Poke two layers
of broken noodles
into the sauce

2 fancy salads

A whole-fennel salad that plays peek-a-boo. And collards with a coconut milk dressing to escape any same-salad rut.

SERVES 4

1 pound (450g) fennel (1 large or 2 small)

3 tablespoons pitted, chopped Castelvetrano olives

2 tablespoons extra-virgin olive oil

1½ teaspoons white wine vinegar

Pinch of red pepper flakes (optional)

Freshly ground black pepper

Zest and juice of 1 lemon 👐 p. 203

Aged provolone, for topping

SHAVED FENNEL SALAD WITH PROVOLONE
from ignacio mattos

1   On a cutting board with a chef's knife, separate the fennel bulb from the stalks and pull off the fronds 👐 p. 169. Coarsely chop the fennel fronds and thinly slice the stalks. Add both to a medium bowl with the olives, oil, vinegar, red pepper flakes, and black pepper to taste. Stir with a serving spoon until well coated.

2   With a mandoline or the chef's knife, slice the fennel bulb crosswise as thinly as you can and add to another medium bowl. Sprinkle the fennel with the lemon zest and juice and stir. Pile the olive mixture in the center of four serving plates, shave the provolone on top with a vegetable peeler, and top each plate with the fennel slices to serve.

SERVES 2 TO 4

¼ cup (60ml) apple cider vinegar

1½ teaspoons sugar

¼ teaspoon fine sea salt

⅛ teaspoon fennel seeds

¼ large Vidalia or red onion, very
thinly sliced 🥄 p. 256

1 bunch collard greens, stems
removed and leaves thinly sliced
into ¼-inch (6mm) ribbons 🥄 p. 48

¼ cup (60ml) full-fat coconut milk

2 tablespoons seasoned rice vinegar

1 tablespoon soy sauce

Pinch of cayenne

COCONUT COLLARD SALAD WITH
QUICK-PICKLED ONIONS

from jenné claiborne

1   To make the pickled onions, about 1 hour before serving, combine the cider
    vinegar, sugar, salt, and fennel seeds in a Mason jar or other sealed container,
    seal, and shake till the sugar dissolves. Add the onion and press down to
    submerge, then cover and set aside for 1 hour at room temperature. These
    keep well in the fridge for 2 weeks.

2   Add the collard ribbons to a large salad bowl. Combine the coconut milk,
    rice vinegar, soy sauce, and cayenne in a small lidded jar, seal, and shake
    aggressively to blend. Pour the dressing over the greens and gently massage
    into the greens to soften them. Top with ¼ cup (60ml) pickled onions to serve.

hands-off dinners for when you want to start cooking, then do other things

THE MOST UNFAIR implication of slow-roasting is the slow part. Because here's the thing: *Fish is always fast.* Its connective tissue and protein structure are more delicate than those of other meats and should generally be cooked as little as possible.

And so, fish is the only case where slow-roasting can take as little as 15 minutes, giving you a beautifully tender, evenly cooked, not-one-bit-dry piece of fish. And if you miss the 120°F (50°C), just-starting-to-flake mark, it will still be good—even carryover cooking after taking it out of the oven won't outrun you, because there isn't much velocity behind it.

Perhaps the simplest, fastest, and most versatile slow-roasting recipe comes from Sally Schneider's cookbook *A New Way to Cook.* All you need: a thin coat of olive oil, salt, and a low oven. She's since discovered that the technique works great for all sorts of fish and shellfish—especially fattier fish like red snapper, striped bass, cod, and even sea scallops—and responds well to all kinds of seasonings (see page 156) and sauces (see page 178).

slow-roasted salmon (or other fish)

from sally schneider

SERVES 4

1 teaspoon extra-virgin olive oil, divided

1 small bunch fresh thyme or other herb sprigs, divided (optional)

1½ pounds (680g) thick, skin-on salmon fillet, or other fish like bass or cod (1 large fillet or four 6-ounce/170g fillets)

Fine sea salt

Flaky salt, chopped fresh herbs, lemon wedges, or a quick sauce 🖐 p. 178, for serving

1   **prep the fish**: Heat the oven to 275°F (135°C) with a rack in the center. Rub a sheet pan lightly with ½ teaspoon of the olive oil. Lay half of the thyme sprigs on the pan and arrange the fish on top, skin-side down. Rub the top of the fish with the remaining ½ teaspoon olive oil, sprinkle lightly with fine sea salt, and scatter the rest of the thyme sprigs on top.

2   **roast the fish**: Roast the fish in the center of the oven until a fork inserted in the thickest part of the fish meets with no resistance and the flesh slides away easily from the skin* and is just beginning to flake when you press down on it with a fork, 15 to 35 minutes, depending on thickness. An instant-read thermometer should read 120°F (50°C). Don't worry if the top of the fish looks a little transparent and raw; this is the result of the low roasting temperature. It will be cooked inside. If any white albumin (coagulated protein) has oozed out, it's an indication your fish may be starting to overcook, but it's harmless.

3   **eat**: Remove the thyme sprigs and serve warm, at room temperature, or cold with a sprinkling of flaky salt and chopped herbs, lemon wedges, or a quick sauce.

  make ahead and store: The salmon will be at its freshest if you eat it sooner than later but will keep in the refrigerator in a sealed container for 2 to 3 days and be delicious plopped cold on top of a salad 🖐 p. 157 or flaked into rice or other grains 🖐 p. 87.

Great with: Coconutty collard salad (page 149) and toasted farro (page 87).

*Crisp That Skin
For crispy salmon skin chips, leave the skin behind on the sheet pan as you lift off the roasted salmon. Heat the broiler with the oven rack 6 inches (15cm) below the heat. Broil the skin on the sheet pan until it's popping and starting to brown, flipping once with a spatula. Let it cool slightly, then crumble over your salmon or just snack away. (And thank Food52er Lune for the idea!)

Slow-roasting isn't that slow—stick this in the oven and dinner's in 20 minutes

Surround with herbs or the other flavor-boosters on page 156 (or nothing)

Is My Fish Done?

Cooking fish at home feels more intimidating than it needs to—because fish is actually *really* good at telling you when it's done.

Just look for the visual cues below in the thickest part of the fillet, and use forgiving cooking techniques like slow-roasting (see page 152). If you're not sure what to buy, I recommend asking the person at the fish counter what's local and freshest (and then cooking it right away) or buying frozen (see thawing tips on page 250), and consulting apps like Monterey Bay Aquarium's Seafood Watch, to see the latest on sustainably caught options.

Here's what your fish is trying to tell you.

VERY RARE

squishy and doesn't flake—this will be more like warm sashimi

MEDIUM-RARE

getting firmer and lighter, but still soft in the middle

MEDIUM

firm but still buttery, flakes with a fork—the 120°F (50°C) sweet spot

VERY DONE

too far, but will be okay—a little drier and stiffer, that's all

Oil the salmon as in step 1 on page 152, then...

Shiitake Snow like *No Recipes* founder Marc Matsumoto:

- Sprinkle lightly with salt, pepper, and onion powder (optional).

- With a Microplane, grate a dried shiitake mushroom like snow all over the salmon for subtle but powerful umami.

- Slow-roast just like in step 2 on page 152.

À la Brisket like *L.A. Times* cooking columnist Ben Mims:

- Salt and pepper the salmon, too.

- In a small saucepan, bring to a simmer over medium-low heat:

  ¾ cup ketchup

  ⅓ cup red wine, such as pinot noir

  2 tablespoons Worcestershire sauce

  2 teaspoons onion powder

  1 teaspoon garlic powder

  1 tablespoon thyme leaves

  4 fresh or dried bay leaves

- Stir constantly with a silicone spatula till the sauce thickens slightly, about 5 minutes.

- Spread the warm glaze over the salmon before roasting in step 2.

Magic Spice-Rubbed like *Korean American* author Eric Kim:

- In a Mason jar, shake together:

  ⅓ cup (65g) dark brown sugar

  1½ tablespoons fine sea salt

  3 tablespoons smoked paprika

  1 tablespoon garlic powder

  1 tablespoon freshly ground black pepper

  2 teaspoons cayenne

  1 teaspoon crushed celery seed.

- Sprinkle over 2 teaspoons per pound (450g) of salmon before roasting (save the rest for sliced cucumbers, boiled eggs  p. 66, and more).

COLD SALMON & POTATOES WITH HERBY YOGURT & PAPRIKA OIL

from emma laperruque

Leftover salmon gets—quickly—*very* exciting in this fancy, minimalist salad from *Big Little Recipes* author Emma Laperruque.

SERVES 2 TO 3

1 pound (450g) small yellow potatoes, halved or quartered

8 cups (1.9L) water

Fine sea salt

¼ cup (60ml) extra-virgin olive oil

1 teaspoon smoked paprika

¾ cup (175ml) whole-milk Greek yogurt, plus more as needed

1 cup (40g) roughly chopped basil or dill, divided

12 ounces (340g) cold leftover salmon ☞ p. 152, broken into big flakes (about 2½ cups)

1 In a large saucepan, bring the potatoes, water, and 1 tablespoon salt to a boil over high heat. Gently boil the potatoes till fork-tender, 8 to 12 minutes. Drain in a colander in the sink and sprinkle with a pinch of salt.

2 In a small saucepan or skillet, heat the olive oil over medium heat. When it shimmers, turn off the heat and use a fork to stir in the paprika and a pinch of salt. With a blender or immersion blender, blend the yogurt and ⅔ cup (25g) of the basil, scraping the sides with a silicone spatula, until the yogurt is bright green and smooth. If you'd like it thicker, stir in a little more yogurt. Add salt to taste.

3 To serve, swoosh the herby yogurt onto dinner plates with a spoon, then top with the cold salmon and warm potatoes. Sprinkle with paprika oil and the remaining ⅓ cup (15g) basil. Save any leftover paprika oil for eggs ☞ p. 14.

SHEET-PAN DINNERS HAVE so much promise: an entire meal prepped in one swoop, roasted and caramelized hands-free—all with just one pan to clean. But many cook unevenly or turn out sleepy and one-note in their haste.

Not here: This recipe—created by *To Asia, With Love* author Hetty McKinnon—is the most flavorful, joyfully textured sheet-pan dinner I've ever made, thanks to hardworking ingredients, brilliantly paired by Hetty. Ready-to-rumble packaged Italian gnocchi form the toasty-chewy base, the hot umami pop of Chinese chili crisp takes care of the seasoning, and a scallion sour cream brightens it all.

sheet-pan gnocchi with chili crisp & baby bok choy
from hetty mckinnon

SERVES 4

GNOCCHI

1 pound (450g) baby bok choy (about 4)

1 to 2 bunches scallions

28 ounces (795g) shelf-stable, frozen, or fresh gnocchi (about 4 cups)*

2 tablespoons extra-virgin olive oil

2 to 3 tablespoons chili crisp, such as Fly By Jing brand, divided

½ teaspoon fine sea salt, divided

Freshly ground black pepper

2 teaspoons toasted sesame oil

1 tablespoon toasted white sesame seeds

½ small lime or lemon, for serving

SCALLION
SOUR CREAM

¾ cup (175ml) sour cream

1 tablespoon extra-virgin olive oil

¼ teaspoon fine sea salt

1 tablespoon lime or lemon juice 🥄 p. 203

1 **get ready to roast:** Heat the oven to 400°F (200°C) with an oven rack positioned in the lower third. Rinse the bok choy well and, on a large cutting board with a chef's knife, slice them lengthwise into halves or quarters—aim for something that looks roughly like page 159. Rinse and trim the tops and bottoms of the scallions 🥄 p. 137. Finely slice 3 and set them aside for the scallion sour cream and garnish. Cut the rest of the scallions in 2-inch (5cm) lengths and set aside with the bok choy.

2 **roast the gnocchi:** To a sheet pan, add the gnocchi, breaking up any clumps, plus the olive oil, 1 to 2 tablespoons well-stirred chili crisp (according to your spice tolerance), ¼ teaspoon of the salt, and a good turn of black pepper. Toss with a wooden spoon to coat the gnocchi, set the pan in the lower third of the oven, and roast for 15 minutes.

3 **make the scallion sour cream:** In a small bowl, whisk together about two-thirds of the finely sliced scallions, the sour cream, olive oil, salt, and lime juice. If the cream isn't thin enough to drizzle, stir in a tablespoon of water at a time until it is.

4 **add the greens:** In a large bowl or tray, stir together the baby bok choy, 2-inch (5cm) scallions, sesame oil, the remaining tablespoon of chili crisp, and ¼ teaspoon salt.

5 After 15 minutes, remove the pan from the oven with oven mitts, carefully stir in the greens, and even everything out to a single layer. Return to the oven until the white bulbs of the baby bok choy are tender when you slide in a fork and the gnocchi are golden underneath, another 10 minutes or so.

6 **eat:** Drizzle with the scallion sour cream, scatter with the remaining finely sliced scallions and sesame seeds, and serve with half a lime to squeeze over top.

store: Leftover gnocchi and sauce keep well in separate sealed containers in the refrigerator for a few days. Crisp up leftover gnocchi in a little olive oil in a nonstick or cast-iron skillet.

Great with: Cold beer or seltzer and cucumber wedges to dunk in the scallion sour cream.

*About That Gnocchi
Gnocchi packages vary—if you end up with slightly more than this, feel free to add it to the pan, or save it to crisp up for a quick meal later in the week (turn the page for another idea).

I DREAM OF DINNER author Ali Slagle keeps shelf-stable gnocchi on hand, not to boil, but to pan-fry golden and crisp. She learned the trick from the legendary Nigella Lawson—who calls them "eight-minute roasted potatoes"—and has since dressed them in everything from lemony cream to pesto to, oh yes: pizza toppings.

In this particular pizza gnocchi, Ali takes the beloved flavors and gooey-crisp-chewy textures of a pepperoni-and-olive slice and deepens them all, with bursting fresh tomatoes, molten mozzarella and Parmesan, and crispy pepperoni not only dotting the top but jagging through the sauce, too.

pepperoni pizza gnocchi
from ali slagle

SERVES 4 TO 6

¼ cup (60ml) extra-virgin olive oil, divided

2 (12- to 18-ounce/340 to 510g) packages shelf-stable potato gnocchi

1 cup (115g) thinly sliced pepperoni

5 garlic cloves, finely chopped ✤ p. 257

Freshly ground black pepper

2 pints (540g) small tomatoes, such as cherry or Sungold

1 cup (135g) kalamata olives, pitted and torn in half

¼ cup (60ml) water

¼ cup (25g) finely grated Parmesan, plus more for serving

¼ cup (10g) thinly sliced or torn basil leaves, plus more for serving ✤ p. 259

Fine sea salt

8 ounces (225g) fresh mozzarella, thinly sliced or coarsely grated

1 **get ready:** Heat the broiler to high, with the rack in the middle of the oven. Prep and gather all your ingredients near the stove—the cooking moves fast.

2 **crisp the gnocchi:** In a 12-inch (30cm) oven-safe skillet on the stovetop, heat 1 tablespoon of the olive oil over medium-high. Add half the gnocchi to the pan, breaking up any that are stuck together. Cover with a lid or sheet pan and cook, without stirring, but using oven mitts to lift the lid and peek occasionally, until golden brown on one side, 2 to 4 minutes. With a wide spatula or slotted spoon, scoop the gnocchi into a medium bowl. Repeat with the remaining gnocchi and another tablespoon of the olive oil.

3 **make the sauce:** Turn down the heat to medium, then add the remaining 2 tablespoons olive oil and most of the pepperoni, saving a handful for the top. Cook, stirring often, until the pepperoni has gone from red to brown and its oil has rendered, 2 to 4 minutes. Stir in the garlic and a few grinds of pepper until the garlic is sizzling. Add the tomatoes, most of the olives (save a small handful for the top), and the water and cook, shaking the pan occasionally, until the tomatoes have softened and most have burst, 4 to 6 minutes. Gently smash the tomatoes if needed to help them along.

4 **pizza-fy it and eat:** Turn off the heat. Add the Parmesan and stir until melted. Stir in the seared gnocchi and basil. Taste and add salt if needed, then shake into an even layer. Top with the mozzarella, the remaining pepperoni and olives, and a hefty grating of Parmesan. Broil until the cheese is melted and browned in spots and the pepperoni is crisp, 4 to 6 minutes. Top with more basil, Parmesan, and pepper and serve hot.

store: Pizza gnocchi's textures will be at their peak on the first day, but leftovers will still be delicious for a few days. Keep in the refrigerator, tightly sealed, and reheat on a sheet pan under the broiler (or eat cold for breakfast, just like its namesake).

Great with: Salty Coke (page 109) and a lemony green salad (page 182).

WHEN WRITER YI JUN LOH'S sister went vegetarian, the long-simmered chicken and pork-based soups that fed their family in Malaysia needed to be rethought. Jun's mom reached for coconut water, which, thanks to its popularity as a healthful, hydrating drink, is easy to find at grocery stores—even gas stations—all over. And unlike packaged boxes of stock, it's made up of just one ingredient that happens to be vegan: the water that comes out of young coconuts, a shockingly good substitute for the umami and subtle sweetness of meaty bone broths.

You can use this trick to quickly give a backbone to any soup or stew, but a good place to start is Jun's riff on his mom's ABC soup, a simple, comforting Malaysian chicken soup, which has not one but two doses of coconut water. The first is subtly steeped with the vegetables; the second remains light and fresh.

one-pot coconut water abc soup

from yi jun loh

SERVES 4 TO 6

4 cups (950ml) water

8 cups (1.9L) coconut water, divided

1 teaspoon fine sea salt

3 medium white or yellow onions, peeled and quartered 🥣 p. 256

4 medium potatoes, peeled and cut into 1½-inch (4cm) chunks (I especially like starchy russets here)

2 medium carrots, peeled and cut into 1-inch (2.5cm) chunks

2 medium tomatoes, quartered (well-drained canned tomatoes are fine)

1 teaspoon crushed white peppercorns, or to taste 🥣 p. 59

1   **about 1 hour before you want soup, simmer the broth**: In a deep pot, combine the water, 4 cups (950ml) of the coconut water, and salt. Bring this to a boil, then turn it down to a simmer.

2   **simmer the vegetables**: Using a colander, strainer, or slotted spoon (to prevent splashing), carefully lower the onions and potatoes into the pot and simmer on very low heat, uncovered, for 30 minutes. Then, add the carrots and tomatoes in the same way and simmer for 20 to 30 minutes more. The vegetables should all be close to falling apart at this point, which is perfect.

3   **season and eat**: Stir in the crushed peppercorns and the remaining 4 cups (950ml) coconut water and bring to a final boil. Season to taste with salt, and serve hot.

make ahead and store: The soup will keep well in a sealed container in the refrigerator for 1 week. Reheat in the microwave or in a pot over medium-high heat on the stovetop until steaming hot.

Great with: Honey-sautéed spinach (page 208) and a cup of tea.

One dose of
coconut water
to flavor the veg,
then another
at the end for
freshness

Also, this is how you add stuff to hot liquids
without burning yourself! Lower it in gently with
something that will keep your hand far away

COCONUT WATER NUOC CHAM

from andrea nguyen

As a kid, cookbook author Andrea Nguyen was the sauce-maker for her Vietnamese family, and she came up with this two-step technique to make sure her nước chấm (or dipping sauce) was in sweet-salty-tangy-spicy balance. More recently, Andrea has been experimenting with coconut water in place of regular water for extra umami and subtle sweetness. Make this for sprinkling over rice (page 105), cold noodles, and roasted vegetables (page 195) or for dunking bites of crisp chicken (page 171) or fish (page 152).

MAKES ABOUT ¾ CUP (175ML)

3 tablespoons lime juice (from 2 limes) 👑 p. 203

2 tablespoons sugar

½ cup (120ml) coconut water

3 tablespoons fish sauce

1 small garlic clove, finely minced 👑 p. 257 (optional)

1 or 2 Thai chiles, thinly sliced, or 1 teaspoon tương ớt tỏi (chili garlic sauce) (optional)

1   Combine the lime juice, sugar, and coconut water in a small bowl, stirring with a spoon to dissolve the sugar. Taste and ask yourself: Does this limeade taste good? Adjust the flavors to balance out the sweet and sour.

2   Add the fish sauce and any of the optional ingredients. Taste again and adjust the flavors to your liking. Aim for a stronger flavor than what you'd normally like, since this sauce will likely be used to add final flavor to foods that will taste better with a little oomph.

make ahead and store: You can make this up to 8 hours ahead—cover and keep at room temperature. (The lime will lose its brightness and get slightly bitter beyond that.)

THIS TECHNIQUE DOES away with all of the unpleasant parts of cooking chicken breasts—the risk of overcooking; the dry blandness of it all; having to slice or pound or sear them. Instead of all that, on his blog *The Hungry Hutch*, *Washington Post* writer Aaron Hutcherson gently cooks the chicken in the simplest and most hands-off way I've ever seen: He slips them whole into a flavorful coconut milk porridge to poach.

While you go about your business, the chicken burbles along, drinking in the flavors of the stew—a method that makes even notoriously lean light meat both very hard to overcook and very easy to shred into bite-size bits after it's done (which is also, conveniently, one way to tell that it's done—see page 170). In this porridge, the chicken takes on coconut, fennel, and ginger, but it could just as easily be a spicy marinara (page 118) or fish sauce-fueled broth (page 114).

chicken fennel quinoa porridge
from aaron hutcherson

SERVES 4

Olive oil

1 yellow onion, sliced
👐 p. 256

1 fennel bulb, sliced, fronds saved for garnish
👐 p. 169

1 pound (450g) carrots, sliced ¼ inch (6mm) thick

2 inches (5cm) fresh ginger, minced (about 1 tablespoon) 👐 p. 260

2 garlic cloves, minced
👐 p. 257

Salt and freshly ground black pepper

1 cup (170g) white quinoa

4 cups (950ml) unsalted chicken stock

1 (13.5-ounce/400ml) can unsweetened coconut milk

2 boneless, skinless chicken breasts

1 **sauté the vegetables**: In a large pot over medium heat, warm a thin layer of olive oil. Add the onion, fennel, and carrots and cook until the vegetables begin to soften, stirring occasionally with a wooden spoon, about 5 minutes.

2 **make the porridge**: Add the ginger and garlic and cook until fragrant, 2 to 3 minutes. Season with a couple pinches of salt and a few grinds of pepper. Add the quinoa, chicken stock, and coconut milk; bring to a boil, then reduce the heat to a low simmer. Taste the broth—it should taste nicely seasoned.

3 **poach the chicken**: Add the chicken, making sure it's completely submerged, and cook uncovered at a low simmer just until the chicken is firm, white, and shreds easily, 20 to 25 minutes 👐 p. 170. An instant-read thermometer inserted into the thickest part should read 165°F (74°C).

4 **shred the chicken and eat**: With oven mitts, remove the pot from the heat. With two forks, pull the chicken breasts out of the pot and set them on a cutting board. When cool enough to handle, shred the chicken with the forks or your hands. Return the shredded chicken to the porridge and stir. Divide among four bowls and top with the reserved fennel fronds to serve.

make ahead and store: The porridge is great made a day or two ahead and refrigerated in a sealed container. To keep the fennel fronds fresh, store them separately in another container lined with a damp kitchen towel or paper towel and sprinkle onto the warm porridge just before serving. Warm up leftover porridge in the microwave or in a pot over medium heat on the stovetop, stirring frequently and adding a splash of water if it gets too thick.

Great with: A bright green salad (page 113)—add some thinly sliced fennel stalks and fronds.

Your cutting board will be covered with colorful veg, <u>not</u> raw chicken—it dives straight into the pot

It's so much easier to make bite-size after its cooked anyway

HOW TO
deal with fennel

So many recipes only use the white, chubby bulb of the fennel, which often leaves you with a bushel of perfectly good stalks and fronds. The stalks are a bit tougher than the bulb, but sliced thinly, they blend right in (check out the salad on page 148). Here's how to dispatch (and eat) every last bit.

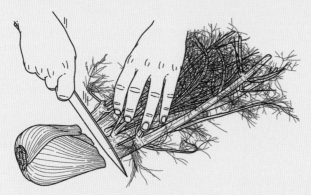

1) Lop off the stalks and bushy green fronds

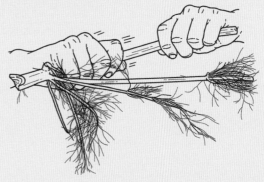

2) Slide the fronds off the stalks (keep the fronds in a container in the fridge with a damp towel—they keep much longer than most herbs)

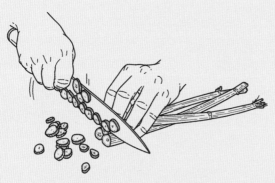

3) Thinly slice the stalks

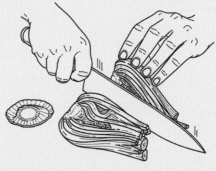

4) Halve the bulb and trim off any bruised spots

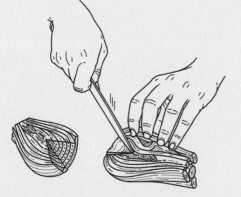

5) Some people trim away the tougher core if eating raw (taste and see what you think!)

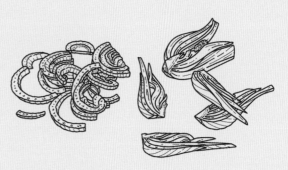

6) Thinly slice the bulb in wedges or half-moons

Cooking Safely with Chicken

Yes, it's important to take care when you cook chicken to avoid any risk of salmonella contamination, but it's easy to do.

Here are the dos and don'ts that will become second nature the more you cook.

- When you're able, buy organic or humanely raised chicken from a local farmer, which is half as likely to be infected with drug-resistant salmonella as conventionally raised chicken.

- Use it soon after buying, within 2 days (and if it smells funky, say goodbye).

- Don't wash it—that will only chicken-up your sink and kitchen.

- Use a cutting board and knife just for the chicken, then wash them well with hot, soapy water. (If you're not using a dishwasher, wooden boards have actually been proven to be more hygienic—wood has natural healing abilities, while plastic boards can get scars that trap bits.)

- Wash your hands after touching raw chicken and any countertops or tools that might have been caught in the crossfire, too.

- Cook chicken till it's done. An instant-read thermometer is great insurance, and so are your own eyeballs— see the chart below for what to look for in both the light meat (breast) and dark meat (thighs and legs).

Is My Chicken Done?

	NOPE	STILL NO	YES!	TOO FAR, BUT WILL BE OKAY
LIGHT MEAT				
DARK MEAT	Squishy, pink, raw	Getting firmer and paler, but still pink	Firm, pale without pink and 165°F (74°C) in the thickest part	Drier and tougher, but l so with a gentle cookin method like poaching slow-roasting

CRISPY CHICKEN THIGHS

from christopher hirsheimer & melissa hamilton

I haven't found a better way to cook juicy, crisp-skinned chicken thighs since sharing this one in the *Genius Recipes* cookbook in 2015—the key is slowly melting the fat locked away in the skin in a barely hot pan. So here it is again, streamlined. I now season the pan, rather than the chicken, to skip dirtying an extra plate and avoid salt skittering across the counter.

SERVES 4

Salt and freshly ground black pepper

8 skin-on, bone-in chicken thighs, patted dry with paper towels

½ lemon, for serving (optional)

1 Sprinkle a light dusting of salt and a few grinds of pepper evenly over the bottom of a large heavy skillet. Lay the chicken thighs in the skillet, skin-side down, in a single layer. Season the top with more salt and pepper.

2 Cook over medium heat without moving until the skin is deep golden brown and releases easily from the pan, about 30 minutes (if it's sticking, give it time—it will release when it's crisped). Reduce the heat to medium-low if it's sizzling quickly or the skin starts to burn.

3 Flip the chicken with tongs and cook until the meat closest to the bone is firm and no longer pink and an instant-read thermometer in the thickest part reads 165°F (74°C), 10 to 15 minutes. Serve the chicken with the hot pan drippings and a squeeze of lemon.

FOR THAT COZY, melting quality we love in braised dishes like ragùs and stews, many recipes will ask you to cut your meat into smallish chunks, sear them on all sides (in batches so you don't crowd the pan), and then nestle them in a saucy liquid to simmer for a few hours till all the connective tissue melts away and the meat falls to bits. But it turns out you can skip some of that.

In this recipe from cookbook author Jenny Rosenstrach's blog, *Dinner: A Love Story* (first shared by her husband Andy Ward with the promising headline "Instant Dinner Party"), you brown and braise a pork shoulder all in one big hunk—it's going to cook for 3 to 4 hours till it falls to smithereens, anyway—then make your sauce right alongside it in the pot. Whatever ragù is left behind is a boon: with pasta, in tacos, on a grilled cheese, or frozen and awaiting more dinners.

pork shoulder ragù (aka the instant dinner party)
from andy ward & jenny rosenstrach

SERVES 6 (OR FEWER, WITH THE BEST LEFTOVERS)

2 to 2½ pounds (900g to 1.1kg) pork shoulder roast (boneless or bone-in)*

Fine sea salt and freshly ground black pepper

2 tablespoons olive oil

1 tablespoon butter

1 small yellow onion, chopped 🖐 p. 256

1 garlic clove, minced 🖐 p. 257

1 (28-ounce/794g) can whole tomatoes (or 2 cans, for a more tomatoey sauce)

1 cup (240ml) red wine

5 sprigs fresh thyme

5 sprigs fresh oregano

1 tablespoon fennel seeds

1 tablespoon smoky hot sauce (such as sriracha or Tabasco)

1 pound (450g) pappardelle or polenta 🖐 p. 175, for serving

Freshly grated Parmesan, for serving

1 **at least 5 hours (or up to 2 days) before you want ragù, prep the pork:** Heat the oven to 325°F (165°C) with the racks positioned so you can slide a Dutch oven or other large lidded ovenproof pot into the middle of the oven. Unwrap the pork and put it on a rimmed sheet pan to catch any flying salt and pepper, then pat it dry with paper towels. If it there are any loose pieces, tie it into a neater bundle with cooking twine 🖐 p. 176.

2 **sear the pork:** Grind a little pile of pepper, about 15 good grinds, to free up your hands, then generously salt and pepper the roast all over with about 1½ teaspoons salt and the pepper.

3 Add the olive oil and butter to the Dutch oven and heat over medium-high on the stovetop just until the butter melts. Using tongs, carefully lower the pork into the pan and brown it well on all sides, about 3 minutes per side. If it ever sticks to the pan, just give it a little more time on that side—once it has a good sear, it should release.

4 **make a flavorful braising liquid:** With the tongs, scootch the pork to the side of the pan and add the onion and garlic. Cook them in the sizzling butter-oil, stirring with a wooden spoon, until they're just softened, about 1 minute. Move the pork back to the middle of the pot, add the tomatoes and their juice, the wine, thyme, oregano, fennel, and hot sauce and bring to a simmer. Cover the pot and, using oven mitts, carefully stick it in the oven.

5 **let it braise for 3 to 4 hours:** Turn the pork every hour or so and check on the liquid levels. (Using oven mitts, you'll need to carefully pull the oven rack partway out, lift the lid off, and use tongs to flip the pork over.) The liquid should be about one-third

continued

*On Shoulders and Butts
Confusingly, pork shoulder (aka picnic shoulder) and butt (aka Boston butt) both come from the shoulder and work great here—the butt will be a little richer. Picnic shoulder sometimes comes with the skin attached, which you'll want to cut away with a paring knife for this recipe (or ask the butcher to do it for you).

pork shoulder ragù (aka the instant dinner party)
continued

of the way up the pork—if it dips below that, add more liquid (water, wine, or canned tomatoes). The meat is done when it's practically falling apart when you poke it with the tongs, 3 to 4 hours. With the tongs, lift the pork onto a cutting board (remove the sprigs of herbs and bone, if there is one, at the same time) and pull the meat apart with two forks. If there's a lot of grease in the pot, you can spoon some off (or, if you're making this ahead, it's extra easy to scrape it off after it's chilled). Then add the shredded meat back to the pot and stir it into the sauce.

6 **eat**: Serve over polenta or tossed with pappardelle or other cooked pasta, loosening the ragù with a little pasta cooking water if needed. Either way, top with lots of finely grated Parmesan from a Microplane.

make ahead and store: Let the ragù cool off in its pot at room temperature till it's not steaming hot (but no more than 2 hours), then stick the covered pot right in the fridge. Before serving, some people like to scrape off a little of the chilled surface fat if there's a lot (though some people leave it *all* to make it extra rich and delicious— your call). About 40 minutes before serving, warm the ragù, covered, over medium-low heat on the stovetop or at 300°F (150°C) in the oven. Hint: Get the rest of dinner ready now. Leftovers keep well (and get even better) in a sealed container in the fridge for 1 week. They freeze well, too—see tips on page 250.

Great with: Garlic toast (page 73) and arugula with lemon, olive oil, and salt.

Sear, simmer, and shred all in one big hunk

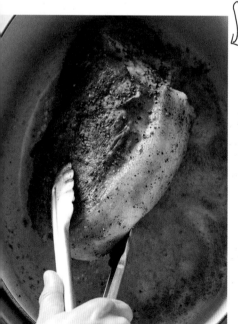
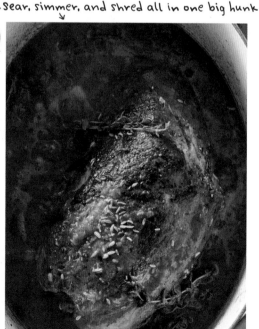

SHORTCUT POLENTA
from maria speck

Traditional polenta means standing and stirring for close to an hour. *Simply Ancient Grains* author Maria Speck's make-ahead method takes only 15 minutes of active cooking (an overnight pause does the rest).

SERVES 8

2 cups (310g) medium-grind cornmeal

3 cups (710ml) boiling water

3 cups (710ml) low-sodium chicken broth (or more water)

1 teaspoon fine sea salt

3 tablespoons unsalted butter

1 cup (100g) finely grated Parmesan, plus more for serving

½ teaspoon freshly ground black pepper

1 **8 hours to 2 days ahead,** add the cornmeal to a large heavy pot and whisk in the boiling water. Cover and let sit at room temperature for at least 8 hours and up to 12 hours. (After that, refrigerate for up to 2 days.)

2 About 20 minutes before serving, add the broth and salt to the pot and whisk to break up big clumps. Bring to a boil over medium-high heat, whisking occasionally. Lower the heat to a gentle simmer, whisking continuously as the mixture thickens, about 2 minutes (if it's spattering, lower the heat further).

3 Cover and simmer over low heat, stirring and scraping the bottom well with a wooden spoon every couple of minutes, until the polenta is creamy and thick, 10 to 12 minutes. The grains of polenta should be tender, with a little chew. For looser polenta, add a little more water or broth. Turn off the heat and stir in the butter, Parmesan, and pepper. Taste, adjust the seasoning, and serve, passing more Parmesan.

store: Leftovers will keep in a sealed container in the fridge for 3 days. To reheat, cut into slices and crisp in butter or olive oil in a nonstick pan over medium-high heat on the stovetop.

When a recipe asks you to truss something, it just means to tie it with food-safe kitchen twine into a neater bundle so there's nothing sticking out that could burn. (Just snip the twine off after cooking.)

There's a fancy way to truss that's a little like playing cat's cradle and will make you feel very crafty and professional. Or there's the lazy way that's impossible to forget. Both work!

THE FANCY WAY:

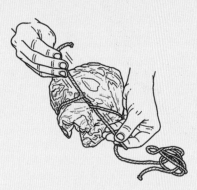

1) Tie the roast once around the top in a double knot, leaving a long tail

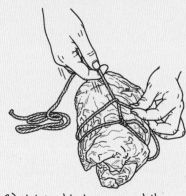

2) Make a big loop around the roast, slipping the tail through to make a T crossing

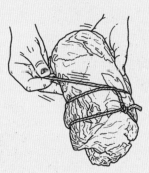

3) Pull tight

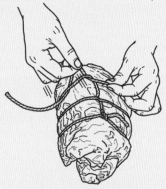

4) Do it again and again, straightening your Ts as you go

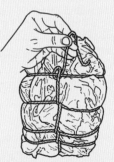

5) Weave it up the back and tie it off

6) Pretty!

THE LAZY WAY:

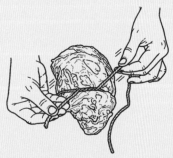

1) Tie a double knot at the top (loop through twice to keep the twine from slipping)

2) Trim the twine and repeat

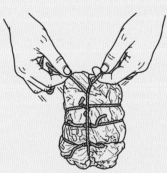

3) Bundle it up the other way. Only slightly less pretty!

common braising woes
(& how to fix them)

If your ragù turns out more like a soup or even a charred mess, it will be okay. Here's what to do for future braising success (and with what's sitting in front of you here and now).

it burned!

THIS TIME
Salvage any that doesn't look blackened. Soak the pot till you can face it again and see "How to Deal with Burnt Pots" (page 263).

NEXT TIME
Get an oven thermometer to make sure you're not running hot (they're cheap and will save your cookies and cakes, too).

Check it earlier, keep adding liquids if the level in the pot drops below one-third of the way up the roast, and make sure it stays at a laid-back simmer.

the sauce is too thin.

THIS TIME
Let it keep simmering on the stovetop (lid off!) to evaporate some of that water.

NEXT TIME
Add more tomatoes or other veg from the get-go (but not more tomato juice).

the sauce is too thick.

ANYTIME
Add a few spoonfuls of water (or more canned tomatoes) till it looks good and saucy to you.

it's been hours and the meat never got tender!

THIS TIME
The sauce is still tasty, right? Eat that with pasta and save the meat for chopping up and serving in tacos, fried rice, or grain bowls later on.

NEXT TIME
Make sure the liquid never boils more wildly than a little blub-blub simmer—that's the braising sweet spot that lets all the meat's connective tissue melt slowly over time.

2 quick, happy sauces

A 30-second raw tomato sauce that whips up as smooth as aioli. And a pico de gallo from the Pacific coast of Mexico that you can make all year, even when there's not a ripe tomato to be found.

SERVES 2

1 ripe tomato (about 170g) or 10 ripe grape or cherry tomatoes

¼ teaspoon fine sea salt

¼ teaspoon freshly ground black pepper

1 tablespoon plus 1½ teaspoons high-quality olive oil

FRESH TOMATO SAUCE
from jacques pépin

1 If using a larger tomato, on a cutting board with a sharp paring knife or serrated knife, cut out the dry scar at the top and then cut the tomato into 1-inch (2.5cm) pieces. With a blender or immersion blender, blend the tomato until smooth, 15 to 20 seconds. Add the salt, pepper, and oil and blend for another 10 seconds.

2 Heat the sauce in a medium microwave-safe bowl in the microwave until warm, about 1 minute. Jacques serves this sauce with crispy-skinned Arctic char or doubles the recipe for a summer soup—it's also delicious with slow-roasted salmon 👑 p. 152 or crispy potatoes 👑 p. 204.

MAKES 3 CUPS (710ML)

2 cups halved and thinly sliced red radishes (about 1 pound/450g)

1 cup (100g) peeled, halved, seeded, and thinly sliced cucumber

1 jalapeño or serrano chile, halved, seeded if desired, and finely chopped, or to taste 🍳 p. 70

1 tablespoon roughly chopped cilantro leaves 🍳 p. 258

3 scallions (white and light green parts only), thinly sliced 🍳 p. 137

2 to 3 tablespoons freshly squeezed lime juice 🍳 p. 203

¼ cup (60ml) neutral oil, such as canola

½ teaspoon fine sea salt

CRUNCHY RADISH PICO
from pati jinich

1   Add all the ingredients to a medium bowl and toss well with a spoon. Let stand for at least 5 to 10 minutes before serving.

2   Either serve right away with chips, over slow-roasted salmon 🍳 p. 152, or with anything that could use some bright crunch. Or make the pico up to 12 hours ahead, cover, and refrigerate, though it will soften over time.

mix & match sides (or dinner, if you eat enough of them)

DON'T LISTEN TO chefs who say you have to learn how to emulsify a vinaigrette perfectly to be a good cook. In *The River Café Cookbook*, Ruth Rogers and the late Rose Gray dressed all their green salads year-round in straight lemon juice and olive oil. You can do this as casually as squeezing the lemon half and shaking the oil right over your plate of baby arugula, as I do for my small family almost every night. Or, when feeding more people, you can follow the recipe below to pre-squeeze and tweak your ratios earlier in the game.

This recipe is also here to say that leaves alone can be just as captivating as the confetti of a chopped salad, if you aim for lettuces that are in season and intensely flavored. Rogers and Gray included their list of dream summer (estiva in Italian) and winter (invernale) greens below. Pick up a few at the farmers market and follow the washing and storage tricks on page 185—they'll brighten your dinners all week.

insalata estiva, insalata invernale

from rose gray & ruth rogers

SERVES 6

SUMMER GREENS

8 cups (1.9L) wild arugula, young beet greens, escarole, cavolo nero, spinach, and Swiss chard (or any combination)

OR:

WINTER GREENS

8 cups (1.9L) dandelion, arugula, radicchio, Belgian endive, young spinach, and lamb's lettuce or any bitter green (or any combination)

OIL & LEMON DRESSING

6 tablespoons (90ml) extra-virgin olive oil

2 tablespoons freshly squeezed lemon juice ☙ p. 203

Fine sea salt, to taste

Freshly ground black pepper, to taste

1 **prep the salad greens:** Pick over the leaves, pulling out any that are wilted or yellowing and discarding them in the compost. For any lettuces with a core, such as radicchio, endive, or escarole, trim away the cores with a chef's knife on a large cutting board. Tear or cut any large leaves into reasonably bite-size pieces. Wash and dry the leaves well ☙ p. 185.

2 **make the dressing:** In a Mason jar or other lidded container, combine the olive oil and lemon juice, plus a pinch of salt and a few grinds of pepper. Seal the jar tightly with the lid, shake it well, and immediately dip a lettuce leaf in to taste. If you'd like it brighter, add lemon juice; mellower, add more olive oil; and add salt and pepper until you like it.

3 **just before serving, toss the salad:** Mix all the leaves together in a large bowl. Give the dressing a shake, then pour over less dressing than you think you'll need. Toss the salad lightly using tongs, a large fork and spoon, or your (clean) hands, and taste a leaf. If you'd like, add a little more dressing, toss, and taste again. Serve right away.

make ahead and store: If you have room in the fridge, keep extra greens in the closed salad spinner with a little water in the bottom—they'll last a week or more. Otherwise, you can refrigerate the clean greens wrapped in a clean, dry towel in a sealed container for about 3 days. Store any leftover dressing sealed in the Mason jar in the refrigerator for a few days and let it come back to room temperature before using, adding a squeeze of lemon to perk it up, if needed.

Great with: Pasta with five-minute tomato sauce (page 118) and garlic toast (page 73).

Some people buy bottled dressing, some just buy a few lemons

Leaves are enough

the secrets to never-gritty, very fresh salad greens (& herbs)

Just running lettuces under water can miss some of their secret grit, no fun to bite into in a salad. This method, which also works well with a salad spinner, frees the dirt, then keeps your greens perky for as long as possible (sometimes a week or more).

1) Swish trimmed greens in a big bowl of cool water

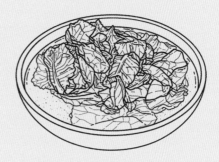

2) Let them sit a couple minutes so all the loosened grit sinks to the bottom

3) Repeat till the water doesn't look dirty, then lift out the greens and lay on clean kitchen towels

4) Roll into a bundle to dry. Store in a clean, dry towel in a sealed container in the fridge for days

common salad woes
(& how to fix them)

Green salads can be a little needy—delicate lettuces want enough dressing to brighten but not overwhelm, and as soon as they're dressed, they start to lose their pep. But don't worry: For pretty much every salad hiccup, there's a cure.

i haven't dressed anything and my lettuces are already wilty!

THIS TIME
Give them a soak in cold water for 15 minutes or so—the water will often help the leaves rehydrate and perk back up.

NEXT TIME
Wash and store your greens as on page 185 not long after you get them home from the market, so they don't have a chance to deflate.

my whole salad is wilty.

THIS TIME
Eat it quick! Slightly softened salad can be delicious, too. Or if it's really too far gone, consider fridging it for a grain salad (page 84) or frittata (page 50) tomorrow.

NEXT TIME
Dress at the last minute and keep lettuces and any other delicate herbs or veg chilled till then.

it's weirdly bland.

THIS TIME
Add more dressing, or just doctor to taste (literally taste bites of lettuce as you go) with a little more salt, pepper, and lemon or vinegar. Or sprinkle with soy sauce, grated hard cheeses, or citrus zest till it tastes great (and move quickly).

NEXT TIME
Consider spritzing it with a little extra lemon juice first to amplify the dressing—a trick used by chefs Bryant Terry (page 188) and Monifa Dayo. Dunk bites of seasoned lettuce in your dressing till they taste great together.

shoot, it's overdressed and soggy.

THIS TIME
Quick! What else can you add in? Another fistful of arugula? A drained can of chickpeas? A couple sliced-up celery stalks?

NEXT TIME
Remember to add dressing little by little and taste as you go, or make the one on page 182, which is good in generous amounts.

3 MORE SMART SALAD DRESSINGS

Miso-Citrus Salad Dressing like *Eat Your Greens* founder Anjali Prasertong:

- Whisk together 2 teaspoons miso paste and 2 tablespoons citrus juice until smooth and creamy. (Anjali recommends white miso paste with orange juice, yellow with lemon, or red with lime—but any combo works.)

- Taste and add more miso or juice as needed.

- Toss with crunchy greens like sliced cabbage or blanched green beans 🥬 p. 101. *Serves 2 to 4*

Tadka Salad Dressing like food writer Annada Rathi:

- In your smallest pot, heat 2 tablespoons olive oil over medium heat for 2 minutes.

- Add ¼ teaspoon black mustard (or fenugreek or nigella) seeds and stay nearby—once the seeds stop popping, take the pot off the heat.

- Let cool, then add:

    2 teaspoons fresh lime juice

    1 teaspoon honey

    ½ teaspoon tahini or peanut butter

    ½ teaspoon mustard

    Freshly ground black pepper, to taste

- Whisk well and serve with any salad, especially with lots of greens, avocado, and nuts. *Serves 2 to 4*

Pantry Salad Dressing like *Roots* author Diane Morgan:

- In a Mason jar, combine:

    1 teaspoon sugar

    1 teaspoon fine sea salt

    Lots of freshly ground black pepper

    ½ cup (120ml) unseasoned rice vinegar

    1½ cups (355ml) extra-virgin olive oil

- Store in the pantry.

- Shake and toss to taste with any salad as is, or flavor it a little differently with every salad: Stir in a little cream, mustard, chopped herbs, spices, and/or grated garlic or Parmesan. *Makes about 16 servings*

ALTHOUGH SMOKY, SLOWLY-SIMMERED collard greens are a delicacy, we can all be eating the greens more often without having to be quite so patient. In his cookbook *The Inspired Vegan*, chef and activist Bryant Terry creates a stunning amount of depth in far less time, without leaning on smoked meat for flavor.

He starts with a dunk in boiling water to soften the greens, then briefly simmers them with white wine, garlic, and, crucially, oven-dried tomatoes—or the contents of an entire jar of meaty sun-dried tomatoes (except for the oil, a bonus genius ingredient in its own right*)—to round off any bitter edges.

white wine–simmered collard greens with oven-dried tomatoes

from bryant terry

SERVES 4 TO 6

Fine sea salt

2 large bunches collard greens, washed and cut into bite-size pieces, ribs reserved 🖐 p. 48

Ice

2 teaspoons extra-virgin olive oil

2 large garlic cloves, minced 🖐 p. 257

1 cup (110g) oven-dried tomatoes 🖐 p. 190 or sun-dried tomatoes, drained and squeezed with a clean kitchen towel (if in oil), thinly sliced*

¼ cup (60ml) white wine

1 **blanch the collards**: In a large pot over high heat, bring 12 cups (2.8L) water to a boil and add 1½ teaspoons salt. Add the collards and cook, uncovered, until softened, 4 to 6 minutes. Meanwhile, prepare a large bowl of ice water to shock the collards.

2 **shock the collards**: Set a colander in the sink. With oven mitts, carefully pour the collards into the colander, then plunge the colander into the bowl of ice water to stop the cooking and set their color. Once cooled, drain the collards well.

3 **sauté the collards**: If you'd like to add the collard ribs, slice them thinly (or save for a future side 🖐 p. 191). In a medium skillet (with a lid or a sheet pan nearby) over medium heat, warm the oil. When it shimmers, add the garlic and cook, stirring with a wooden spoon, until the garlic has softened and the smell has gone from sharp to mellow, about 1 minute. If you're using the sliced collard ribs, add them now and cook until tender, 2 to 3 minutes. Add the drained collard greens, tomatoes, and ⅛ teaspoon salt and sauté until well-combined, about 3 minutes.

4 **simmer and eat**: Add the white wine, stir, cover, and cook for 15 seconds. Turn off the heat and steam for a few minutes. With oven mitts, lift the lid and season with additional salt to taste, if necessary. Serve hot.

make ahead and store: The chopped collards and sliced, dried tomatoes can be prepped a day or two ahead and stored in separate sealed containers in the refrigerator. The cooked collards will keep well in a sealed container in the fridge for 1 week. Reheat in the microwave or in a skillet over medium heat on the stovetop, stirring frequently and adding a splash of water if they start to stick.

Great with: Toasted grains (page 87) and soy-seared tofu (page 117).

continued

*Save That Oil
Arati Menon, editorial lead for Home52, likes to use the oil left from a jar of sun-dried tomatoes to stir-fry vegetables, swirl into hummus, and spoon over soups and omelets—anywhere you'd use olive oil, with a little shout of extra umami. And Nice Dream Ices founder Coral Lee sticks olives or chunks of feta right into the jar to marinate.

to make your own oven-dried tomatoes: At least 8 hours before you want collards, heat the oven to 200°F (95°C). Line a sheet pan with parchment paper or a silicone baking mat. Cut as many fresh, ripe tomatoes as you like in half lengthwise (or in wedges if using large tomatoes) and place cut-side up on the pan. (Two pounds/900g Roma tomatoes will make about 1 cup/110g oven-dried tomatoes, for example.) Feel free to snuggle them close if you're making a lot. Bake until the tomatoes have shrunk and dried, and taste as sweet and concentrated as you'd like, about 8 hours. Store in a sealed container in the refrigerator for 1 week (or in the freezer for longer).

Your very own oven-dried tomatoes (or store-bought work, too)

QUICK-SAUTÉED STEMS
from bryant terry

Recipes that tell you to remove the stems of dark leafy greens are forgetting to mention one thing: Those stems are delicious with just a little heat and time. Slice and cook them for a couple of minutes before the greens for extra pops of texture (and no waste). Or hang onto them in the fridge till you need a green side, like this all-purpose recipe from Bryant Terry's cookbook *Vegetable Kingdom.*

MAKES ABOUT 1 CUP (240ML)

2 teaspoons extra-virgin
olive oil

½ teaspoon minced
garlic 🥄 p. 257

2 cups (200g) thinly sliced
collard, turnip, mustard,
kale, or other dark, leafy
green stems

Salt

½ large lemon

1 In a large skillet, add the oil and garlic and cook over medium heat just until the garlic starts smelling fragrant and mellow, stirring often with a wooden spoon, 2 to 3 minutes.

2 Add the stems and a pinch of salt and cook, stirring often, until tender, about 3 minutes. Season with more salt to taste, then squeeze over the lemon. Add to a soup, stew, or bowl of beans or grains for extra texture, or serve as a side.

MUSHROOMS ARE SOME of the food world's biggest pranksters. When you add them to oil in a skillet, their spongy fungi bodies at first drink up as much as you throw at them. This can lead to a frenzy of adding more and more fat to the pan, until suddenly they collapse and release it all. *Gotcha.*

A common solution is to sear them hot and fast, in small batches with plenty of space in the pan, so they brown before they have a chance to start playing tricks. But this tactic really limits how many mushrooms you get to eat. In chef Millie Peartree's much more efficient recipe, she lets the roaring heat of the oven sear a big batch all at once, then wilts in a mountain of soft greens, too. Both shrink so much that you can start them packed closer together than you usually would with roasting veg (see page 195): The mushrooms will have plenty of room to brown once they've cooked down a bit, and the greens—never big crispers—will softly twirl through.

sheet-pan roasted mushrooms & greens
from millie peartree

SERVES 4

½ cup (60g) dried cranberries (optional)

1 pound (450g) cremini mushrooms (or a mix of mushroom types)

3 small shallots, sliced 🥄 p. 207

4 garlic cloves, chopped 🥄 p. 257

2 tablespoons olive oil, plus more as needed

¼ teaspoon fine sea salt

Freshly ground black pepper

¼ teaspoon red pepper flakes

10 ounces (285g) soft greens (spinach, arugula and/or mustard greens), washed, stemmed, and chopped, if needed 🥄 p. 48

1   **get prepped**: Heat the oven to 425°F (220°C). In a small bowl, soak the cranberries in hot water until plump, about 10 minutes, then drain. Meanwhile, wash and dry the mushrooms 🥄 p. 194. On a cutting board with a chef's knife, trim any tough, dry bottoms of the mushroom stems and slice creminis or other thicker mushrooms ¼ inch (6mm) thick.

2   **roast the mushrooms**: On a 13 by 18-inch (33 by 45cm) sheet pan (or two smaller sheet pans), toss together the mushrooms, shallots, garlic, and olive oil with your hands. Season with the salt and a few grinds of pepper and spread in an even layer (it's okay if they're overlapping a bit). Roast until golden brown and crispy, 15 to 20 minutes, scraping and stirring once with a spatula halfway through for even browning.

3   **wilt the greens on top**: With oven mitts, take the sheet pan out of the oven and set it on a couple of cool burners of the stovetop. Pile the red pepper flakes and greens on top of the mushrooms and gently stir them into the mushrooms with the spatula. If you're struggling to stir, don't worry—it will get easier after it wilts in the oven a bit. With the oven mitts, return the pan to the oven to roast until wilted, about 5 minutes, stirring once after 2 minutes and drizzling with a little more olive oil if the greens or mushrooms look dry. Add the drained cranberries, taste, and tweak the seasoning as needed. Serve hot or at room temperature.

store: The mushrooms and greens keep well in a sealed container in the refrigerator for a week. They're delicious mixed into pastas and grains and make any eggs instantly feel all dressed up.

Great with: Creamy scrambled eggs (page 10) and toast.

A Briny Boost
If you have dill pickles in the fridge, steal 2 tablespoons of their brine and add it in step 3 along with the greens, like State Bird Provisions chef Stuart Brioza does with his mushrooms. They won't taste pickly, just mysteriously brighter and more alive.

wash (yes, wash) mushrooms

The rumor has been that you should never let water get near your mushrooms and instead tenderly wipe each one clean with a damp towel. This is a good way to spend 20 minutes losing all desire to eat mushrooms. America's Test Kitchen, bless their hearts, tested how much water mushrooms truly absorb and proved this rumor bunk. Wash away.

1) Hose them under running water (with a spray nozzle if you have it), rubbing with your hands to loosen any dirt

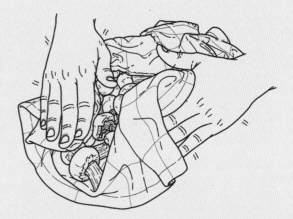

2) Pat dry with a clean kitchen towel

3) Slice, chop, and so on (stems are usually tasty and only need any dry, hard ends trimmed, though tough ones like on shiitake and portobello should go)

salt is enough

but other spices are cool, too →

a thin coat of oil to help brown

← space for hot air to move (and steam to escape)

only extras that are thick enough not to burn (and easy to pick out if they do)

what any roasting vegetable should look like

Whether you're roasting broccoli or butternut squash, the same method works—it will just take more or less time, depending on how big and dense the vegetable is (see the timeline below to guesstimate).

THE GO-TO FORMULA: 425°F (220°C) oven + thin coat of oil + pinch of salt + enough space to brown = delicious roasted vegetables. (Millie Peartree's mushrooms and greens on page 192 can crowd because they shrink a *lot* as they roast, and benefit from some softness.)

A few more tips:

- Check halfway through roasting, rotate the pans if you have more than one, and stir—that bottom tray likes to secretly burn underneath.

- If anything is sticking, leave it till it crisps up, then jimmy it up with a spatula. (Or line the pan with a silicone baking mat or parchment for insurance.)

- Pierce the veg with a fork to check if it's tender—and don't forget to taste, season, taste!

How Long Stuff Takes to Roast, give or take*

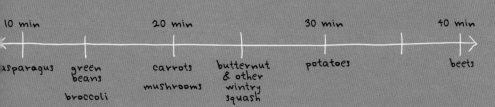

10 min		20 min		30 min		40 min
asparagus	green beans	carrots	butternut & other wintry squash	potatoes		beets
	broccoli	mushrooms				
	cauliflower					
	brussels sprouts					

*in ½-inch (1.3 cm) chunks in a 425°F (220°C) oven, depending on how soft you like them

mix & match sides (or dinner, if you eat enough of them) **195**

ROASTED BUTTERNUT SQUASH recipes tend to ask us to peel and cube (and, therefore, wrestle), almost by default. But here's the easiest way to peel a butternut squash: *Don't.* "Generally, if I'm roasting a squash, I won't bother peeling it first," chef and author Yotam Ottolenghi wrote to me. "Butternut squash skin is actually incredibly delicious when roasted as it gets quite sticky and chewy in a way I particularly enjoy." In fact, nearly every cookbook he's published has at least one recipe with hunks of roasted, unpeeled squash in it, including this one from *Jerusalem*, his cookbook with Sami Tamimi of recipes inspired by the city where they both grew up.

To get that sticky-good skin, the way you roast matters: They hack the squash into big chunks, then position them so their skin crisps and blisters against the hot sheet pan. If instead you really want a supersmooth texture, like in a soup or mash, feel free to peel, though Ottolenghi still recommends doing so after cooking, when the peels have naturally loosened.

roasted butternut squash & red onion with tahini & za'atar
from yotam ottolenghi & sami tamimi

SERVES 4

1 large butternut squash (about 2.4 pounds/1.1kg), scrubbed and cut into ¾ by 2½-inch (2 by 6cm) wedges 👐 p. 199

2 red onions, peeled and cut into 1-inch (2.5cm) wedges 👐 p. 256

3 tablespoons plus 1 teaspoon (50ml) olive oil, divided

Fine sea salt

Freshly ground black pepper

3½ tablespoons well-stirred tahini*

1½ tablespoons freshly squeezed lemon juice* 👐 p. 203

3 tablespoons water

1 small garlic clove, minced 👐 p. 257

Scant ¼ cup (30g) pine nuts

1 tablespoon za'atar

1 tablespoon roughly chopped parsley 👐 p. 258

1. **roast the vegetables**: Heat the oven to 425°F (220°C). To a large bowl, add the squash, onions, 3 tablespoons of the olive oil, ½ teaspoon salt, and a few grinds of pepper and toss well with your hands. Arrange on a sheet pan (or two, if needed) skin-side down and spaced well apart 👐 p. 198, and roast until the vegetables have started to brown and are tender when a knife is inserted, about 40 minutes, using oven mitts to rotate the pans halfway through if using two. Heads up: If the onions finish faster than the squash, transfer them with tongs to a platter and continue roasting the squash. With oven mitts, remove the pan from the oven and let cool to room temperature.

2. **make the sauce**: In a small bowl, whisk together the tahini, lemon juice, water, garlic, and ⅛ teaspoon salt until the sauce is the consistency of honey, adding more water or tahini as needed.

3. **toast the pine nuts**: Pour the remaining 1 teaspoon olive oil into a small frying pan over medium-low heat. Add the pine nuts and a pinch of salt and fry, stirring often, until the nuts are golden brown, about 2 minutes. Pour the nuts into a small bowl.

4. **eat**: To serve, spread the vegetables on a platter and drizzle with the tahini sauce. Sprinkle the pine nuts on top, then the za'atar and parsley. Serve at room temperature.

make ahead and store: You can roast the vegetables and make the sauce a day ahead. Store in sealed containers in the fridge and bring to room temperature before serving. Toast the pine nuts and chop the parsley the day you're serving. The nuts can hang out on the counter; the parsley should be covered with a damp towel in the fridge. Any leftovers will keep in a sealed container in the fridge for a few days.

Great with: Buttermilk-marinated roasted chicken (page 76) and lemony greens (page 182).

*On Half Tablespoons
A half tablespoon equals 1½ teaspoons, but feel free to eyeball here.

No need to peel squash when you blister its skin against a hot pan like so ↘

⌐ The onions might cook faster, but they're easy to snag out if they do

the easier way(s) to slice hard squashes

For how casually we're asked to break down butternut and other hard winter squashes, they can sometimes be so difficult to hack up that some cooks resort to just dropping them on the floor. Cookbook author Virginia Willis has a gentler way, rocking the squash to help ease the knife through.

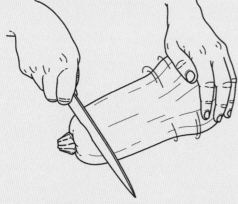

1) Rock the squash back and forth on the cutting board with one hand while letting the knife sink in with the other

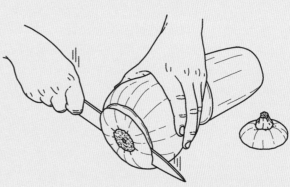

2) Cut off the top and bottom, and—for butternut—slice at the point where the straight neck meets the rounder belly

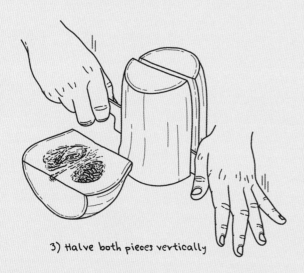

3) Halve both pieces vertically

4) Scoop the seeds from the belly, then slice, flattest-side down, into ¾ by 2½-inch (2cm by 6cm) pieces for fat, Ottolenghi-style wedges

A FEW MORE TIPS:

- If this still isn't working for you, some people also microwave their squash or simmer it in boiling water for a few minutes to soften the outer layer, before letting it cool enough to cut.

- Cookbook author Meera Sodha roasts the whole squash simply pricked in a few places with a fork—plunk it on a sheet pan at 400°F (200°C) and roast until a knife can easily slide in, 1 to 1½ hours. Breaking it down is just as effortless; the insides will be steamy-soft rather than caramelized, which is great for a mash or soup.

SWEET POTATOES BENEFIT from steaming to break down their stringy fibers—but there's no need for a simmering pot of water or steamer basket. In molecular-biologist-turned-food-writer Nik Sharma's cookbook *The Flavor Equation*, Nik splits raw sweet potatoes open, smears them with soft butter, then covers them tightly to steam in the water trapped within their own cells (plus bonus melting butter). Halfway through steaming, he whips off the cover, flips the potatoes onto their cut faces, and lets them roast and caramelize against the hot roasting pan. Why? As Nik discovered, "Roasting produces at least seventeen more aromatic molecules than are achieved through boiling or microwaving, and most of them in higher concentrations." The resulting slabs are the creamiest sweet potatoes I've made at home, with the deepest and most developed flavor.

baked sweet potatoes with maple crème fraîche
from nik sharma

SERVES 4

4 small orange-fleshed sweet potatoes (each around 7 ounces/200g), such as Garnet or Jewel

2 tablespoons unsalted butter, at room temperature

Fine sea salt

1 lime

½ cup (120ml) crème fraîche or sour cream

1 tablespoon maple syrup or honey

2 teaspoons fish sauce (optional, and available vegan)

½ teaspoon freshly ground black pepper

1 scallion

2 tablespoons roasted peanuts

1 teaspoon mild, flavorful ground chile, such as Aleppo, Maras, or Urfa

1 **prep the sweet potatoes**: Heat the oven to 400°F (200°C). Rinse and scrub the sweet potatoes under running tap water. Slice them lengthwise and set them in a roasting pan or sheet pan, cut-side up, with at least 1 inch (2.5cm) of space around each. Using a table knife, smear the cut sides with the butter and season with a pinch of salt. Cover the pan snugly with a lid, sheet pan, or piece of foil pressed around the edges to seal.

2 **roast the sweet potatoes**: Bake for 20 minutes (or about 10 minutes longer, if your sweet potatoes are much bigger than 7 ounces/200g). Using oven mitts and tongs, carefully remove the foil and flip the sweet potatoes cut-side down. Return to the oven and cook, uncovered, until a knife inserted into the center of the largest sweet potato slides through easily, about 20 minutes (or longer for bigger sweet potatoes). Remove from the oven and let rest for 5 minutes.

3 **make the dressing and garnish**: With a Microplane, grate ½ teaspoon lime zest 🥄 p. 203 and set it aside to garnish the potatoes (feel free to leave it right on the Microplane). Squeeze 1 tablespoon lime juice into a small bowl. Add the crème fraîche, maple syrup, fish sauce, and black pepper to the bowl, and whisk until smooth. Taste and season with salt. Rinse the scallion and trim away just the scruffy top and bottom, then slice it thinly 🥄 p. 137.

4 **eat**: Drizzle the warm roasted potatoes with a few spoonfuls of the dressing. Sprinkle with the scallion, peanuts, ground chile, and reserved lime zest. Serve with the extra dressing on the side.

make ahead and store: Roast the sweet potatoes and keep them warm in a low oven (around 200°F/95°C), covered, for up to an hour. Make the dressing earlier in the day and store it in a sealed container in the fridge. The lime zest and scallion are freshest prepped not long before serving. Without the toppings, leftover sweet potatoes keep well in an airtight container in the fridge for a week. The dressing will, too. Other toppings will lose their zip in the fridge, so plan to eat them quickly.

Great with: Soy-seared tofu (page 117) and crunchy veg to dunk in the sauce.

First a buttery (covered) steam to break down their fibers

Then an (uncovered) roast to create at least seventeen more types of flavor molecules

zest & juice the most out of lemons & limes

This is how zesting and juicing *should* happen: zest, *then* juice. It's much easier to hold onto the whole fruit and scrape off just the thin, fragrant outer layer with a Microplane than to do the same with a juiced-out husk. But sometimes recipes don't play out that way or we forget. But don't worry: You can make it work either way. Here are a few more tips.

1) Aim for smooth, heavy lemons and limes that give a little when you squeeze

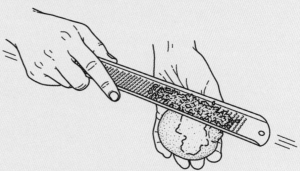

2) Zest with a Microplane above the fruit to catch it all (or use a vegetable peeler, then chop the zest finely)

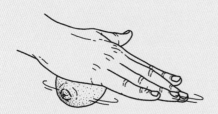

3) Roll under your hand to loosen the juice

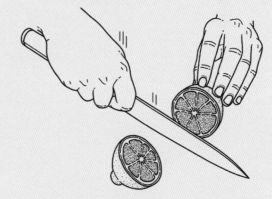

4) Slice in half crosswise

5) Squeeze with a juicer, reamer, or fork to help break out more juice

6) Scoop or strain out any rogue seeds

IF YOU'RE WONDERING why you'd go to the trouble of boiling potatoes and then roasting them, when the oven alone could technically do the job, I was with you—until I tried this recipe. As *Girl Meets Farm* star Molly Yeh explains, boiling in salty water first seasons the potatoes inside and out, but maybe more importantly, it brings a rough, dry layer of the potatoes' starches—or more specifically, a dehydrated layer of gelatinized starch—to the surface, so they get even crispier in the oven. No soggy home fries here.

Molly's paprika mayo is unreasonably good for how simple the ingredients are. It makes double what you need—feel free to halve it, but you'll be glad to have extra to smear on sandwiches, dress salads, and dunk vegetables and chips in all week.

roasted potatoes with paprika mayo
from molly yeh

SERVES 4 (PLUS EXTRA DRESSING)

Salt and freshly ground black pepper

2 pounds (900g) red potatoes, scrubbed and cut into ½-inch (1.3cm) cubes

2 tablespoons unsalted butter, melted*

1 cup (220g) mayonnaise

¼ cup (60ml) white vinegar

1 tablespoon paprika

2 teaspoons sugar

2 to 3 tablespoons minced shallot, to taste ☞ p. 207

Chives, for garnish

1 **boil the potatoes**: Heat the oven to 450°F (230°C). Bring a large pot of well-salted water (it should taste quite salty, almost like seawater) to a boil. Add the potatoes (lower them in carefully with a colander or large strainer ☞ p. 164 to prevent splashing) and cook until slightly fork-tender but not falling apart, 6 minutes. Using oven mitts, strain the potatoes into a colander in the sink, then toss the potatoes back into the empty, still-hot pot briefly to help some of the moisture steam away.

2 **roast the potatoes**: Scatter the potatoes on a sheet pan and season with salt and pepper. Drizzle the melted butter over the potatoes and toss to coat using a wide spatula. Roast until the potatoes are dark brown and crispy, 30 to 45 minutes, tossing halfway through. If the potatoes are sticking stubbornly, don't mess with them—let them keep browning and crisping till they release from the pan.

3 **meanwhile, make the dressing**: In a small bowl, whisk together the mayonnaise, vinegar, paprika, sugar, and shallots. Finely slice the chives and set aside.

4 **eat**: When ready to serve, toss the warm potatoes with half of the paprika mayo (save the rest for salads, sandwiches, and dips). Taste and adjust, top with the chives, and serve.

store: The roasted potatoes (dressed or not) are crispiest and creamiest the day you make them, but leftovers will keep in a sealed container in the fridge for a few days. Crisp them up in a nonstick skillet to reheat, adding a little olive oil if they're looking dry. Extra paprika mayo keeps well in a sealed container in the fridge for a week.

Great with: Smashburgers (page 106) and shishito-style green peppers (page 94).

*Melting Butter, Two Ways (Also, Chocolate)
Cut in small chunks. Then melt 1) over lowish heat in a small pot on the stove or 2) in 15-second bursts in a bowl in the microwave, stirring in between.

⤷ After boiling, a layer of gelatinized starches is ready to get extra crispy

Have faith: Once they get nice, crispy bottoms, they'll release ↗

what exactly did you mean by shallot? (& how to mince it)

Each whole shallot contains multiple lobes that can be all sorts of different sizes, just like garlic cloves—and recipes don't always explain just how much shallot you'll want in the end.

What you can always do is think about the shallot you *want* to be eating. If it's going raw and sharp in a salad dressing, you might mince it a little finer and use a smaller lobe. If you plan to sauté it in butter till it's mellow and rich, a larger cut is probably fine, and you can throw in a lot more. Mincing it is just like chopping an onion (see page 256), in miniature.

1) With a sharp paring knife, trim just the hairy bit off the root end

2) Slice in half lengthwise

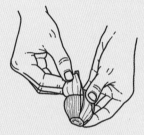

3) Peel away the skin (the knife can help lift stubborn papery bits)

4) Lay one half flat and trim the dried-out tip

5) Carefully make even horizontal cuts about ¼ inch (6mm) apart, leaving the root end intact to hold it all together

6) Next up: a row of vertical slits, again leaving the root intact

7) Chop off even rows crosswise, moving toward the root

8) Leave as is or, for raw uses like dressing, run the knife through a bit more to mince to smithereens

2 superfast green sides

Greens wilted not in butter or oil
but in molten honey. And scallions
as a stand-alone side that needs no salt.

SERVES 2

1 bunch (300g)
spinach leaves

1 tablespoon honey

Salt

HONEY-SAUTÉED SPINACH
from yi jun loh

1   Wash and dry the spinach 👁 p. 185. Heat the honey in a large skillet over medium-high
    heat until it bubbles.

2   Add the spinach and a pinch of salt and cook, stirring occasionally with tongs or a
    wooden spoon, until the spinach is completely wilted, about 2 minutes. Taste and
    tweak the salt and serve hot.

SERVES 2 TO 4

2 bunches scallions (or as many as you'd like to cook)

1½ tablespoons unsalted butter

SKILLET SCALLIONS
from edna lewis

1   Find a large skillet and lid or sheet pan. Wash the scallions, pulling off any wilted outer layers 👁 p. 137. Don't bother drying—a little water will help them steam. With a chef's knife on a cutting board, cut off the hairy roots, then cut the tops down to fit the skillet.

2   Heat the (empty) skillet over medium heat and add the butter. When it melts and foams, add the scallions and cover the skillet. After 3 minutes, with oven mitts, lift the lid and turn the scallions over with tongs. Continue to cook, covered, until the white part is a bit crisp and the tops are tender and shiny, about 2 minutes more. Serve hot—you won't need salt or pepper.

desserts anyone can make

THE STANDARD COOKIE method printed on the chocolate chip bag tells us to soften the butter, which means waiting for a vague not-too-cold, not-too-warm sweet spot, and works best in an electric mixer, not by hand. You won't get *bad* cookies if you miss the mark, but there's too much secrecy and room for error—when we could be skipping it all.

Seven Spoons author Tara O'Brady has been tinkering with her chocolate chip cookie recipe since high school and likes to instead pull the butter straight from the fridge and *melt* it for a denser, chewy-crispy cookie (that happens to be easier to make the moment you want one). Do as Tara does: Bake one tray right away and keep the rest of the dough frozen for an even-more-instant treat another day.

basic, great chocolate chip cookies
from tara o'brady

**MAKES ABOUT
28 COOKIES**

1 cup (225g) unsalted butter, cut into ½-inch (1.3cm) chunks

12 ounces (340g) semisweet or bittersweet chocolate

3¼ cups (415g) all-purpose flour 🍵 p. 215

1¼ teaspoons baking powder 🍵 p. 254

1 teaspoon baking soda 🍵 p. 254

¾ teaspoon fine sea salt

1½ cups (320g) packed light brown sugar

½ cup (100g) granulated sugar

2 large eggs

2 teaspoons vanilla extract

Flaky sea salt, for sprinkling (optional)

1 **get prepped**: Heat the oven to 360°F (180°C) with a rack in the center (350°F/175°C is fine if that's the closest your oven can do). Line two sheet pans with parchment paper. In a medium saucepan over low heat, slowly melt the butter. (You shouldn't hear sputtering.) Stir occasionally with a silicone spatula until the butter is almost melted. Meanwhile, on a cutting board with a chef's knife or serrated knife, chop the chocolate, aiming for a mix of ⅓-inch (8mm) to ½-inch (1.3cm) pieces, with some finer bits.

2 **mix dry, mix wet**: In a medium bowl, whisk together the flour, baking powder, baking soda, and fine sea salt. Grab a large bowl, add the melted butter, and whisk in both sugars. It might look clumpy at first, but it will smooth out quickly. Break the eggs in one at a time, whisking briskly after each one, just until the streaks of egg white disappear. Whisk in the vanilla.

3 **mix dry into wet**: With the silicone spatula, stir the dry ingredients into the wet until the flour is mostly mixed in. Stir in the chocolate, scraping the sides and bottom of the bowl to catch any loose bits, stopping as soon as the flour has disappeared. (Mixing longer will toughen the cookies.)

4 **roll the cookies**: If the dough feels warm or looks glossy, refrigerate it for 5 minutes. Scoop 3 tablespoons dough (55g) per cookie and roll into a ball between your palms. Place 3 inches (7.5cm) apart on one of the lined sheet pans.

5 **bake the cookies**: When one sheet pan is full, sprinkle each ball with a small pinch of flaky salt, if you like, and slide the pan into the center of the oven. Bake until the tops are cracked and lightly golden but still soft in the middle when pressed very lightly with a finger, 10 to 12 minutes, rotating the pan with oven mitts halfway through baking 🍵 p. 214. Let the cookies cool on the sheet pan for 2 minutes, then use a wide spatula to move them to a wire rack to cool completely. Continue shaping and baking cookies with the remaining dough, using a cool sheet pan for each batch.

make ahead and store: The dough balls can be frozen in a sealed container for 3 months. Bake without defrosting at 330°F (165°C)—they may need an extra minute or two. Keep baked cookies sealed on the counter (and eat soon).

What gooey, Chewy & Crispy Cookies Look Like When They're Done

One of the trickier parts of cookie baking is deciding when to take them out of the oven so they're perfect for *you*. More often than not, if they look exactly as golden and crisp as you want them to be while still in the oven, they'll veer hard and crunchy by the time they've cooled. (This is another good argument for not baking all your cookies at once—more chances to zero in on your own just-right.)

While every cookie has its own quirks, this visual guide to Tara O'Brady's chocolate chip cookies (page 212) will give you a sense of the control you have over your cookie's destiny.

8 MINUTES	11 MINUTES	14 MINUTES

in the oven: smooth and not yet dry on top

in the oven: tops cracked and lightly golden

in the oven: deeply browned

↓ ↓ ↓

after cooling: gooey and collapsing

after cooling: crisp on the edges, chewy and soft in the middle

after cooling: extremely crunchy—bash these up in a bowl of milk for cookie cereal

the best (& second-best) way to measure flour

Because flour and other powdery ingredients like cocoa powder can settle differently every time you scoop a cup—depending on how packed the flour was in the bag, the humidity, whether small children are nearby—weighing your ingredients on a digital scale will always be the most consistent way to land not-leathery-dry, *just-right* baked goods. (Plus there are other benefits, like dirtying fewer dishes.)

But if you don't have a scale yet, or you're separated for whatever reason, the Spoon and Sweep Method will give you a happy-medium, slightly fluffed cup that should work well in any of the desserts in this book (and is also a good place to start with other recipes, unless the author tells you otherwise).

HERE'S THE BEST WAY (AND THE RUNNER-UP):

How to measure by weight:

The labels might vary slightly with your brand of scale, but the basic process should be the same.

1) Set your bowl on the scale and turn it on (it should say 0)

Hit the grams/ounces button to switch units, if needed

2) Add flour till it hits the weight you're looking for

3) Hit "tare" to zero it out and move along to the next ingredient

How to measure by volume (Spoon and Sweep Method):

1) give the flour a couple of stirs in the bag or container to loosen slightly

2) Spoon the flour into your measuring cup

3) Scrape across the top with the back of a table knife, letting the extra fall back in

IN SO MANY baked goods, removing the flour would be like taking the walls off a house: It would no longer be recognizable, or all that good. Even in brownies, where stiff structure isn't a hallmark, flourless versions usually have to compensate with other absorbent, binding ingredients like cornstarch or almond flour.

But Genevieve Ko, author of *Better Baking*, knows that many brownie recipes already contain a flour-like ingredient that won't dilute the flavor: cocoa powder. So, during her time as cooking editor of the *Los Angeles Times*, she found the right ratio to increase the cocoa and scrap the flour entirely. The recipe she came up with is pure, shiny-topped chocolate and is likely to convert anyone who thinks they're Team Cakey or Team Chewy into a fudgy brownie person.

flourless fudgy brownies
from genevieve ko

MAKES ONE 8 INCH (20CM) SQUARE PAN

Nonstick cooking spray or neutral oil, for the pan

½ cup (113g) unsalted butter

1 cup (180g) semisweet chocolate chips

⅔ cup (139g) sugar

½ cup (48g) natural unsweetened cocoa powder 👓 p. 215

⅛ teaspoon fine sea salt

3 large eggs, at room temperature*

OPTIONAL ADD-INS

½ cup (95g) chocolate chips (any type, optional)

¾ cup (75g) walnuts, toasted and coarsely chopped 👓 p. 261 (optional)

1　**get prepped**: Heat the oven to 325°F (165°C). Line the bottom and sides of an 8-inch (20cm) square pan with foil and lightly coat the foil with nonstick cooking spray (or rub it all over with a little neutral oil).

2　**melt the chocolate**: In a medium saucepan, melt the butter and chocolate chips over low heat, stirring occasionally with a silicone spatula, until smooth. Turn off the heat, slide the saucepan to a cool burner, and let cool to room temperature.

3　**make the batter**: Meanwhile, in a large bowl nestled in a damp kitchen towel to steady it, whisk together the sugar, cocoa powder, and salt. If the cocoa is lumpy, sift the mixture through a fine-mesh sieve, pressing through any lumps, then dump any salt left in the sieve into the bowl, too.

4　Break the eggs into the bowl and whisk just until smooth (but not so long that they get frothy). While whisking, steadily pour in the cooled melted chocolate until smooth. If adding more chocolate chips or walnuts, stir them in now (or sprinkle the chocolate chips on top of the batter once it's smoothed in the pan). Pour the batter into the lined, oiled pan and smooth the top with the spatula.

5　**bake the brownies**: Bake until a toothpick or long, dry noodle inserted in the center comes out with moist crumbs clinging to it 👓 p. 218, 30 to 35 minutes. Cool in the pan on a wire rack or cool stove burner, then grab the edges of the foil and lift out onto a cutting board. Peel off the foil, cut, and serve immediately (or freeze for 30 minutes to 1 hour first to cut neater squares).

make ahead and store: The brownies keep well in a sealed container at room temperature for 5 days or in the freezer for 3 months.

*On Room Temperature

When you forget to take the eggs out of the fridge to come up to room temperature, just set them in a bowl of lukewarm water (not hot or they'll cook!) while you get everything else ready.

Is My Cake (or Brownie) Done?

Your first clue that your cakes and brownies are done will usually be a sweet, toasty scent tugging you to check the oven. But then you'll want to peek to see if the top is dry and firm when you gently poke the center with a finger, and the edges have pulled away from the sides of the pan (though be sure to look for the cues mentioned in the recipe, as other specific traits might be more important).

A toothpick poked in the center will help seal the deal—and yes, a toothpick (or other rough-textured tool, like a dry spaghetti noodle) is usually a more sensitive indicator than a smooth-sided cake tester or knife, though any will work in a pinch. Here's what we mean if we say it should come out with just moist crumbs clinging.

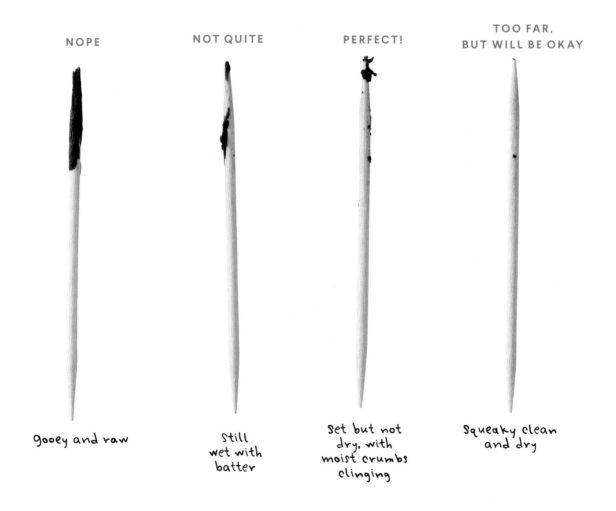

NOPE

NOT QUITE

PERFECT!

TOO FAR,
BUT WILL BE OKAY

gooey and raw

Still
wet with
batter

Set but not
dry, with
moist crumbs
clinging

Squeaky clean
and dry

3 MORE WAYS YOUR BROWNIES CAN DRESS UP

Make the brownie batter on page 216 through step 4, then . . .

Raspberry-Lime Swirls like *Grandbaby Cakes* author Jocelyn Delk Adams:

- With a blender or immersion blender, blend ½ cup (60g) fresh or frozen raspberries with 1½ teaspoons freshly squeezed lime juice until smooth (if using frozen, let them soften slightly to blend, but don't completely defrost).

- Dollop onto batter and swirl into tart, bright pockets with a toothpick or table knife before baking.

Malty Sprinkles like *Women on Food* author Charlotte Druckman:

- Before baking, sprinkle over a generous dusting of malt powder, like Ovaltine, Carnation, or Milo, for a toasty, milky flavor (think: Whoppers) and crystalline crunch. (Chocolate malt flavor is also good, as pictured below.)

- Note that the brownies will not be gluten-free if you add malt powder, which has wheat and barley extracts.

Fancy Chocolate Bar Chunks like Nice Dream Ices founder Coral Lee:

- Find a chocolate bar with intriguing inclusions, as they say in the biz, like cocoa nibs or candied ginger or nuts.

- Chop or break into jagged chunks and partially submerge them in the top of the batter before baking to stretch their flavors and textures further.

IN THESE FROTHY shakes, chef Millie Peartree leans on two of the plant world's greatest magic tricks: frozen banana's ability to whip up like soft-serve ice cream, thanks to its natural pectin, and the fact that a rich, whippable cream floats to the top of cans of cold full-fat coconut milk.

This means that, with bananas in your freezer and coconut milk in your fridge, you will always be about 10 minutes from a gleeful dessert for just about everyone you want to treat: vegan, gluten-free, lactose-intolerant, and other limited diets alike. And importantly, it will feel like plan A, not an afterthought, as everyone gulps it down.

banana shakes with coconut whipped cream
from millie peartree

SERVES 2

1 (13.5 ounce/400ml) can full-fat coconut milk or coconut cream

2 tablespoons confectioners' sugar, sifted through a sieve if clumpy, or to taste

2 teaspoons pure vanilla extract, divided

4 medium ripe bananas, sliced and frozen (about 350g frozen slices)*

1 to 1¼ cups (240 to 300ml) dairy-free milk of your choice (depending on desired consistency)

2 tablespoons creamy peanut butter (optional)

Cinnamon, for sprinkling (optional)

1   the night before, remember to chill the can for the coconut whipped cream: Stick the can of coconut milk or cream in the refrigerator. Do not shake the can, especially if using coconut milk (you're trying to separate and solidify the cream layer, so you can scoop it out and whip it).

2   at least 30 minutes before serving, get your equipment chilly: Chill a medium mixing bowl and whisk or the beaters of an electric mixer in the freezer for 30 minutes or more.

3   right before serving, whip the cream: Use a spoon to scoop the hardened coconut cream 🥄 p. 222 into the chilled mixing bowl and leave all clear liquid behind (feel free to use this in your banana milkshake!). Whip the cream by hand with the chilled whisk (or faster with an electric mixer), until the cream thickens and light peaks form, about 1 minute. (Note that it may not whip up as much as dairy whipped cream, and that's okay! It is its own delicious light, frothy treat.) Sweeten the cream with confectioners' sugar and whisk in 1 teaspoon of the vanilla extract.

4   blend the shakes: With a blender or immersion blender, blend the bananas, dairy-free milk, remaining teaspoon vanilla, and peanut butter until smooth.

5   drink: Pour into two tall glasses and top with coconut whipped cream and a sprinkle of cinnamon, if you like.

make ahead and store: The shakes are best drunk right away, but you can cover and refrigerate the coconut whip for up to 3 days. It will likely thicken a little more as it chills.

*About Those Bananas

Whenever you have too many ripe bananas, peel and slice them into chunks and throw them into a zippered bag in the freezer. (Peeling frozen bananas can be done but will make your hands very cold!)

Frozen bananas blend as creamy as soft-serve

That top layer of cold coconut cream is highly whippable (the rest is for your milkshakes)

AVOCADO PALETAS
from fany gerson

Creamy avocados star in this naturally vegan, gluten-free Mexican dessert from *Paletas* author Fany Gerson.

MAKES 8 TO 10

1 cup (240ml) water

½ cup (100g) sugar

2 small ripe avocados

Pinch of salt

2 tablespoons freshly squeezed lime juice 👆 p. 203

4 ounces (115g) bittersweet chocolate, chopped (optional)

2 tablespoons coconut oil (optional)

1   **At least 5½ hours ahead,** in a small saucepan, stir the water and sugar with a silicone spatula over medium-high heat, until the syrup comes to a boil. Let cool to room temperature.

2   On a cutting board with a paring knife, cut the avocados in half lengthwise around the pit. Remove the pit 👆 p. 28 and scoop the flesh out with a spoon. With a blender or immersion blender, blend the avocado, cooled syrup, and salt until smooth, scraping the sides as needed. Add the lime juice and blend just until combined.

3   Pour into ice-pop molds or glasses, stick in ice-pop sticks, and freeze until solid, about 5 hours. If using glasses, freeze until the paletas are beginning to set, 1½ to 2 hours, then insert the sticks and freeze until solid, 4 to 5 hours.

4   Optionally, for a chocolate shell: In a microwave-safe bowl, melt the chocolate and coconut oil 20 seconds at a time, stirring after each till smooth. Let cool to room temperature.

5   Remove the paletas from the molds, dipping the outsides briefly in warm water if needed to loosen, then dunk in or drizzle with the chocolate.

THIS FRENCH YOGURT cake is so simple, cookbook author Dorie Greenspan explains in *Baking: From My Home to Yours*, that in France it's typically measured by scooping up flour, sugar, and oil right in the yogurt container. But yogurt comes in different sizes in the United States, so Dorie worked out a version of the recipe that could be re-created worldwide, either by weight or with measuring cups and spoons.

Pinching the citrus zest and herbs into the sugar is both therapeutic and memorable: It's a genius trick you can take to other recipes to send good smells floating through your kitchen and, ultimately, your cake. As I was writing this book, Dorie had just taught this blueberry, lemon, and thyme riff for a kids' cooking class, but feel free to get creative with other berries, citrus, and herbs (and see more ideas from Dorie on page 227).

blueberry-thyme yogurt cake

from dorie greenspan

SERVES 8

Softened butter or baker's spray, for the pan

1½ cups (204g) all-purpose flour 👐 p. 215

2 teaspoons baking powder 👐 p. 254

¼ teaspoon fine sea salt

1 cup (200g) sugar

1 to 2 teaspoons finely chopped thyme 👐 p. 258

1 lemon

½ cup (120ml) plain yogurt, at room temperature 👐 p. 226

3 large eggs, at room temperature 👐 p. 216

½ cup (120ml) oil, such as canola or olive oil

1 cup (150g) blueberries

Lightly sweetened crème fraîche, for serving (optional)

1 **get prepped**: Heat the oven to 350°F (175°C) with a rack in the center. Generously butter the inside of an 8½ by 4½-inch (21 by 11cm) loaf pan (or coat it with baker's spray). If your pan is ½ inch/1.3cm bigger all around, that's okay—check the cake a little earlier as it might bake faster.

2 **mix dry, mix wet**: In a small bowl, whisk the flour, baking powder, and salt together. To a medium bowl, add the sugar and thyme and finely grate the zest of the lemon over it with a Microplane (save the naked lemon in the fridge for salads and use within a few days, before it dries out). Working with your fingertips, rub the ingredients together until the sugar is moist and aromatic. Whisk in the yogurt until it's thoroughly incorporated, and then add the eggs one at a time, blending each egg into the batter before you add the next. When all the eggs are in, give the mixture a few energetic beats to bring it all together.

3 **mix dry into wet**: Switch to a silicone spatula and stir in half of the flour mixture. When it's well incorporated, add the remaining flour and stir until blended. Add the oil to the bowl gradually, stirring and scraping the bottom and sides until you have a thick, smooth batter with a light sheen. Drop the berries into the batter and stir to mix them in evenly. Scrape the batter into the buttered pan, smoothing the top.

4 **bake the cake**: Bake the cake in the center of the oven until the cake is golden brown and starts to pull away from the sides of the pan and a toothpick or long, dry noodle inserted deep into the center of the cake comes out clean or with moist crumbs clinging 👐 p. 218, 55 to 60 minutes. With oven mitts, take the cake out of the oven and set on a wire rack or cool stove burner. Wait 5 minutes, then run a table knife between the cake and the sides of the pan to loosen the cake. Carefully invert the pan onto the rack, then flip the cake so it's right-side up and finish cooling to room temperature. Serve with lightly sweetened crème fraîche, or nothing at all.

make ahead and store: The cake keeps best well-sealed at room temperature; it will be good for at least 4 days. It can also be frozen for up to 1 month—defrost, still sealed, at room temperature.

Pinching zest and herbs into sugar ↗
with your fingers helps the citrusy
smells travel through your cake

A highly conductive (i.e., metal)
bowl set in warm water helps hustle
your yogurt to room temp (stir here
and there—and try not to splash)

Skip the blueberries and thyme on page 224 and . . .

For Dorie's original French Yogurt Cake from *Baking*:

- Swap in 1 cup (125g) all-purpose flour plus ½ cup (55g) ground almonds for the all-purpose flour, for a slightly richer, deeper flavor.

For Dorie's Riviera variation in *Baking*:

- Use thick Greek yogurt, olive oil, and orange (or mandarin or tangerine) for the zest. (Thyme is still good, or try rosemary.)

Jam-Belly Cupcakes:

- Line a 12-cup muffin pan with paper liners or butter the cups.

- Put a large spoonful of batter into each cup, drop in a teaspoon of jam or marmalade, and cover with more batter, filling no more than two-thirds full.

- The baking time will be shorter, 20 to 25 minutes. Cool and, if you'd like, top with frosting  p. 240 or whipped cream.

IN THE COMFORTING family of cold, creamy custards and puddings, this popular Puerto Rican dessert is among the very simplest to make at home—and one that, unlike many, sidesteps dairy, eggs, and gelatin to be completely vegan. Thanks to the thickening power of cornstarch, it can be whisked together in moments from your pantry, then left alone to chill for a few hours and get good and wobbly.

Tembleque comes from the verb temblar, which means "to shake" in Spanish, "a wonderful name that refers to its trembling, wiggly texture, like panna cotta or flan mixed with Jell-O," as writer and radio producer Von Diaz explains in her cookbook *Coconuts and Collards*. Von encourages playing with other tembleque flavors like almond or lemon extract or dried lavender, strained out after cooking. And once you have orange flower water and cinnamon in your cupboard, you're halfway to the North African orange salad on page 231, too.

tembleque
from von diaz

SERVES 10, AND SCALES
UP OR DOWN WELL

½ cup (65g) cornstarch

½ cup (100g) sugar

¼ teaspoon fine sea salt

1 teaspoon orange flower
water (agua de azahar)

4 cups (950ml) full-fat
coconut milk (from three
13.5-ounce/400ml cans)*

Ground cinnamon,
for garnish

1 **at least 5½ hours (and up to 1 day) before you want tembleque, mix the base:** In a large saucepan, whisk together the cornstarch, sugar, salt, and orange flower water. While whisking, slowly pour in the coconut milk and whisk until everything is well combined.

2 **heat the tembleque:** Heat the saucepan over medium-high heat, stirring continuously with a silicone spatula, until the mixture starts to thicken. Lower the heat to medium and continue stirring until the mixture just barely starts to boil. Turn the heat off, slide the pan to a cool burner, then immediately pour into either small heatproof cups or bowls or a 9-inch (23cm) wide, 3-inch (7.5cm) tall pan, scraping with the spatula to get all of the tembleque out of the pot.

3 **cool the tembleque at least 5 hours (or up to 1 day):** Allow the tembleque to cool at room temperature until just warm, about 1 hour, then cover with reusable beeswax wrap or foil and refrigerate until cold, at least 4 hours.

4 **eat:** It's easiest to just sprinkle the cinnamon on top of the tembleque and serve. Alternatively, if you want to show off its trembling texture even more, loosen the edges with a table knife and flip the tembleque out into individual bowls or onto plates (for the small cups) or a large serving plate (for one larger pan) before sprinkling with cinnamon.

store: Any leftover tembleque will keep in a sealed container in the refrigerator for 3 days. It may start to crack, but it will still taste delicious.

*About That Coconut Milk
Aim for a brand with only coconut in the ingredients. You'll have a little left over—save it for iced café de olla (page 49) or oatmeal (page 18). Von also recommends making fresh coconut milk when you have access to fresh mature coconuts.

Pour in the coconut milk slowly to avoid lumps

Cook just a few minutes to thicken (then wait patiently a few hours to set till trembly)

SALADE D'ORANGES
from dr. jessica b. harris

With orange flower water and ground cinnamon in your pantry, you can make both Tembleque (page 228) and this bright orange salad from Algeria—shared by culinary historian Dr. Jessica B. Harris in *The Africa Cookbook*—any time you like.

SERVES 6 TO 8, AND SCALES UP OR DOWN WELL

12 Valencia oranges

2 tablespoons orange flower water

1 teaspoon ground cinnamon

3 tablespoons confectioners' sugar

1 On a cutting board with a paring knife, slice off the top and bottom ½ inch (1.3cm) of the oranges and slice the peel away, curving around the outside 🍵 p. 142 (or simply peel them with your hands as you would to eat). Slice the oranges crosswise into thin circles, and nudge out any seeds with the tip of the paring knife.

2 Lay the orange slices, slightly overlapping, on a large platter (or in a shallow glass bowl). Sprinkle the orange flower water over the oranges. In a small bowl, stir the cinnamon and confectioners' sugar together with a spoon, then sprinkle over the oranges. You can either eat the salad right away or, for an even more refreshing and flavorful dessert, cover tightly with reusable beeswax wrap or plastic wrap and chill for 30 minutes before serving.

WHEN YOU FREE pie from its pan and do away with lattices and other frilly toppers, what you end up with, counterintuitively, is pie in both its most beautiful and drama-free form. And even if you've never considered making pie dough and it scares you a little, you can do this—the photos on pages 236–237 will show you how.

These free-form, intentionally rustic pies are called galettes in French or crostatas in Italian, and, as long as your dough stays good and cold and your oven very hot, there's little that can go wrong (and for anything that does, there's a fix—see page 235). This galette, from *Great British Bake-Off* star Benjamina Ebuehi, includes a few extra bits of insurance. Benjamina mixes the dough together with a table knife to avoid stirring up extra gluten—you want just enough to hold nice, big pockets of cold butter that will poof into flaky layers in the oven, but too much can toughen the crust.

She also sprinkles the rolled-out dough with almond flour before piling on the fruit, to drink up the bubbling juices and protect the bottom crust from getting too soggy. But even if some of the juices escape, the sticky syrup that pools on the parchment will only make the galette look more striking and care-free.

peach galette
from benjamina ebuehi

SERVES 6 TO 8

CRUST

7 tablespoons (100ml) ice-cold water

1 tablespoon plus 1½ teaspoons apple cider vinegar or freshly squeezed lemon juice 🥄 p. 203

1½ cups (180g) all-purpose flour 🥄 p. 215

½ teaspoon fine sea salt

1½ teaspoons superfine sugar (or granulated sugar)

½ cup (110g) unsalted butter, cut in ½-inch (1.3cm) cubes and chilled

ingredients continued

1   **at least 3½ hours before you want galette, make the dough**: In a measuring cup, mix together the ice-cold water and vinegar and set it near where you'll be working, along with a tablespoon. In a large bowl, stir together the flour, salt, and sugar with your fingers. Add in the cold, cubed butter and quickly rub it into the flour with your fingertips until you have a coarse mixture with some pea-size chunks of butter and some smaller ones 🥄 p. 236.

2   Drizzle 1 tablespoon at a time of the cold vinegary water onto the flour, then stir with a table knife—do this just until the dough starts to clump together (if you squeeze a small handful, it should hold its shape instead of crumbling apart). You may not need to use all of the water.

3   **chill the dough at least 2 hours**: Lightly flour the flat surface where you'll be rolling your dough (a large cutting board or clean section of your counter), then tip the dough onto it and gently gather and press the dough into a round disk shape—it doesn't need to be completely smooth. Wrap the dough in a reusable beeswax wrap or plastic wrap and chill in the fridge for at least 2 hours, until firm. Leave the surface floury—you'll be rolling again soon.

continued

peach galette
continued

FILLING

1½ pounds (680g) peaches (about 5 ripe peaches)*

¼ cup (50g) lightly packed light or dark brown sugar

2 teaspoons vanilla extract

1½ teaspoons ground ginger

1 tablespoon cornstarch

Squeeze of lemon (about 1 teaspoon)

2 tablespoons plus 1½ teaspoons ground almonds

GLAZE

1 egg, beaten with a fork

1 tablespoon Demerara sugar (or granulated sugar)

2 tablespoons maple syrup

4   **meanwhile, make the filling**: On a cutting board with a paring knife, cut the peaches in half, working your way around the pit, then scoop out the pit with a spoon. Slice the peaches about ½ inch (1.3cm) thick. In a large bowl, stir together the peaches, brown sugar, vanilla, ground ginger, cornstarch, and lemon juice until evenly combined. Set aside.

5   **roll out the dough**: Line a sheet pan completely with parchment paper. Once your dough has chilled for 2 hours, unwrap it onto your lightly floured surface, with a little pile of extra flour nearby. Rub a rolling pin or a straight-sided bottle (like a wine bottle) with flour and roll out the dough into a large circle, 12 to 13 inches (30 to 33cm) in diameter and about ¼ inch (6mm) in thickness, rotating the pastry a quarter turn after every couple rolls to prevent sticking and to keep the circular shape. If at any point the dough gets sticky, set it on a plate or sheet pan and chill in the fridge for 10 to 15 minutes, until firmer again.

6   **start assembling the galette**: Gently fold the dough in half, brushing away any loose flour you can with a pastry brush or your fingers. Lift the dough onto the center of your lined sheet pan, flipping it floury-side up if you can (this way, any lingering flour can help the filling thicken instead of toasting on the bottom). Sprinkle the ground almonds evenly across the center of the dough, leaving about 2 inches (5cm) clear along the edge.

7   **fill and chill**: Pile the peaches in an even layer on top of the almonds, again leaving a thick border around the edge. Moving around the circle with your fingertips, fold the overhanging edges of the dough up over the peach filling 👁 p. 237. Set the sheet pan in the fridge to chill for 20 minutes. Heat the oven to 375°F (190°C).

8   **bake the galette**: With a pastry brush or your fingers, brush the top of the dough with the beaten egg and sprinkle with the Demerara sugar. Bake the galette until the crust is golden brown, 45 to 50 minutes. In the last 2 to 3 minutes of baking, with oven mitts, remove the galette from the oven and glaze the peaches with the maple syrup using a pastry brush or spoon. Return the galette to the oven for the remaining few minutes to heat the glaze through.

9   **eat**: Remove from the oven and let the galette cool for a few minutes. Eat at any temperature you like.

make ahead and store: Well-wrapped, the dough can be chilled for a week or frozen for 3 months. Baked galette is at its best on day one, but leftovers will keep well in a sealed container at room temperature for a day or so, or in the fridge for a few days longer (and it makes an excellent breakfast).

Or Any Fruit, Really
If you can't find fresh peaches, frozen also work really well, or feel free to riff with other combinations of fruit: peach-raspberry, all the berries, straight apple—you name it.

common pie dough woes
(& how to fix them)

Pie dough doesn't have to be scary. (And a cold beer can't hurt.)

the dough is a melty mess!

THIS TIME

At any stage, stick it in the fridge (either wrapped up or on a plate or sheet pan) until it firms up again.

NEXT TIME

Move quickly and keep everything cold (even your flour and bowl, if it's warm in your kitchen).

my chilled dough is now rock hard and unrollable.

THIS TIME

Let it rest at room temperature for 15 minutes or so. It's okay to slam it with the rolling pin, too.

NEXT TIME

Roll out within a few hours of chilling (or rest and slam, as above).

my dough is too crumbly to roll out.

THIS TIME

As you roll, flick a few little drops of water over the driest areas. It should start to come back together.

NEXT TIME

Make sure the dough holds together when you clench it in your hand before chilling it (see page 236).

uh-oh, i'm getting holes/weird amoeba shapes as i roll.

THIS TIME

That's okay! Trim outlier pieces to patch the holes.

NEXT TIME

Roll from the center outward, turning the dough often, and feeling the thickness around the edges as you roll. This will become second nature very soon.

my filling leaked everywhere!

THIS TIME

I hope you lined your pan well, but if you didn't, see page 263 for tips on de-sticking the pan.

NEXT TIME

If your fruit looks super juicy, consider holding some of the juices back, or adding more almond flour buffer.

butter seeped out from my crust!

THIS TIME

Serve warm with ice cream—no one will notice.

NEXT TIME

Stop working in the butter when you have lots of pea-size chunks, and chill the dough well.

how the heck do i clean this up?

Scrape the floury counter with a bench scraper or stiff spatula. Throw the bits in the trash, not the sink (it'll stick and isn't great for the drain). Wipe the counter with a soapy sponge. Now you get to eat pie!

THE KEYS TO peach galette

1) Start with really cold butter

2) Quickly pinch and rub until it looks like this ↗
(a mix of pea-size and smaller bits)

3) Stir in ice-cold water with a knife ↗
till it holds together like this

↖ 4) Press into a disk, then wrap
and chill 2 hours

5) Roll from the center out
(a wine bottle works just fine)

6) Give it a quarter turn every few
rolls to help keep it from sticking

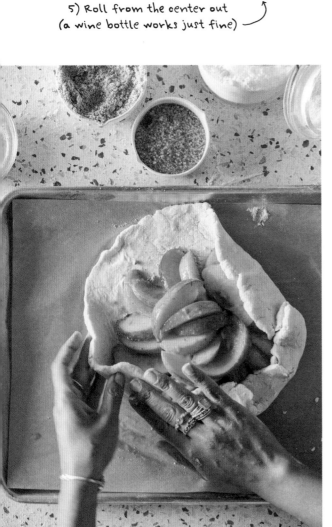

7) Fold over the edges (unlike fancy lattice crusts,
it will look stunning no matter what)

8) Done! Beautiful!

IF YOU'VE EVER wanted to make a loved one a birthday cake and quickly felt overwhelmed by the decision-making (why are there so many kinds of buttercream?) or the equipment and expertise many recipes assume, you are, emphatically, not alone. Stacking cakes on top of each other isn't something most of us practice often, and every time we do, it's for a crowd.

But this one, from Julia Turshen's cookbook *Small Victories*—a plush, deeply chocolatey number, and a favorite of her wife, Grace—can be whisked together in a couple of bowls without any special machinery. The step-by-step illustrations on pages 242–243 will help, too.

The frosting is a formula you'll memorize—equal parts room temperature sour cream and melted chocolate, sweetened with maple syrup—and does just as well in swoops and swirls as it does sleek and smooth: "Whatever makes you happy," as Julia says.

happy wife, happy life chocolate cake
from julia turshen

MAKES 1 TWO-LAYER 8-INCH (20CM) CAKE

CAKE

Softened butter, for the pan

1¼ cups (150g) all-purpose flour ☙ p. 215

1 cup (200g) sugar

¾ cup (75g) Dutch-process cocoa powder (such as Guittard or Droste), sifted if lumpy ☙ p. 215

1 teaspoon baking soda

1 teaspoon baking powder

¼ teaspoon fine sea salt

½ cup (110g) unsalted butter, melted and cooled ☙ p. 204

2 eggs, lightly beaten

1 cup (240ml) strong black coffee, at room temperature

1 cup (240ml) buttermilk or plain yogurt

1 teaspoon vanilla extract

ingredients continued

1 **at least 3 hours before you want cake, get ready to bake**: Heat the oven to 350°F (175°C) with a rack in the center. Use your hands to butter the insides of two 8-inch (20cm) cake pans,* then line the bottom of each with a circle of parchment paper ☙ p. 241. Butter the parchment paper.

2 **make the batter**: In a large bowl, whisk together the flour, sugar, cocoa powder, baking soda, baking powder, and salt. Add the melted butter, eggs, coffee, buttermilk, and vanilla and whisk until smooth. Divide the batter evenly between the two lined, buttered cake pans, scraping the bowl with a silicone spatula to get all the batter into the pans. (A rough way to do this is to scoop the batter 1 cup/240ml at a time into each pan until you run out, or, more precisely, to weigh the batter—but eyeballing is also fine.)

3 **bake the cake**: Put the two pans on the center rack of the oven with a little space between them and bake the cakes, switching their spots in the oven using oven mitts halfway through for even baking, until the cakes are firm to the touch and a toothpick or a long, dry noodle inserted into the center of each cake comes out clean or with crumbs clinging ☙ p. 218, about 30 minutes.

4 With oven mitts, take the cakes out of the oven and set them on a wire rack or cool stove burners to let them cool completely in their pans, about 30 minutes. Once cool, run a table knife around the edges and flip the pans onto a clean work surface to remove the cakes (you might need to give the pans a little thump with the heel of your hand). Peel off and discard the parchment.

continued

*About Those Cake Pans
If you have only 9-inch (23cm) pans, that's okay—they'll bake quicker so check early. Or if you have only one cake pan, as long as it's at least 3 inches (7.5cm) tall, you can bake one big cake (it will take a bit longer), then cool and slice it into layers with a serrated knife.

happy wife, happy life chocolate cake
continued

FROSTING

¾ cup (130g) semisweet chocolate chips or roughly chopped semisweet chocolate

¾ cup (180ml) sour cream, at room temperature
👁 p. 226

1 tablespoon maple syrup

½ cup (160g) raspberry jam

Raspberries, for serving (optional)

5 **make the frosting**: Bring a small pot half-full of water to a boil and then lower the heat to a simmer. Put the chocolate chips in a large stainless steel or heatproof glass bowl and set it on top of the pot (the water should not touch the bowl—if it does, carefully pour a little down the drain). Stir the chocolate with a silicone spatula until the chocolate is melted. (Alternatively, microwave the chocolate in a microwave-safe bowl 15 seconds at a time, stirring in between.) With oven mitts, take the bowl off the heat, set on a towel or a cool burner on the stove, and whisk in the room-temperature sour cream and maple syrup until very smooth. Cover and refrigerate the frosting to let it thicken until the cakes have cooled.

6 **stack the cake**: Once the cakes are cool, put one on a serving platter with the flat side (the bottom) facing up. If you want the platter to stay tidy, tuck strips of parchment under the edge of the cake 👁 p. 241. Spread the jam over just the top with a small offset spatula or table knife. Stack the second cake on top of the jam-smeared cake, again flat-side up. (If the layers slide around, use a couple of skewers to hold them together while you frost the sides, then remove the skewers to frost the top.)

7 **frost the cake**: Using a small offset spatula or table knife, spread the frosting all over the sides and top of the cake. Don't worry about making it perfect—Julia likes it rustic-looking. But if you want it super smooth, go ahead.

8 **let it rest**: Let the cake sit for about 1 hour before serving to let the jam really seep in and the flavors meld. Julia even prefers to make it the day before, refrigerate it overnight, and serve it cold. Either way, slice and serve with some fresh raspberries alongside, if you'd like.

make ahead and store: Bake the layers a day ahead and keep tightly covered at room temperature (or freeze, tightly wrapped, for 1 month—defrost at room temperature, still wrapped). Make the frosting a few hours ahead, cover, and chill. Or make the whole thing the day before, refrigerate, and serve cold like Julia does. Leftovers will keep well in the refrigerator for 3 or 4 days.

3 MORE WAYS TO RIFF LIKE JULIA

For a vanilla cake, leave out the cocoa powder and coffee. Easy!

For cupcakes, line a standard 12-muffin pan with paper liners, scoop in the batter (no more than two-thirds full), and bake until firm to the touch, about 20 minutes. Top with raspberry jam or frosting.

For a speedy vanilla frosting, whip ½ cup (120ml) very cold heavy whipping cream until it holds a stiff peak, then gently fold in ½ cup (120ml) room-temperature sour cream. Add confectioners' sugar to sweeten to your taste and a splash of vanilla extract.

For parchment paper circles to help your cake slide out, cut 8-inch (20cm) squares, fold a few times, then cut a rounded edge

Parchment wings can help keep your platter tidy, too

HOW TO
stack a layer cake with confidence

Whenever I'm worried that the food I'm sharing won't look good, I remember something Julia Turshen once said, "I decided I'd rather be relaxed than pretentious." It's a choice—and an empowering one—to embrace simplicity rather than flash and perfection. This cake and frosting are especially forgiving, however fancy (or not) you choose to make them.

1) grab a big plate and a few strips of parchment paper

2) Position the bottom cake, flat-side up

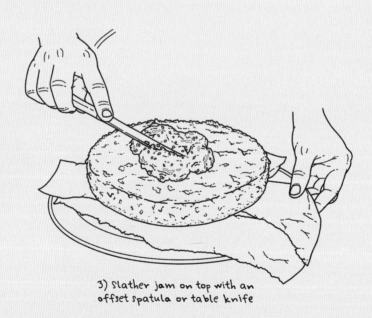

3) Slather jam on top with an offset spatula or table knife

4) Stack the top cake, flat-side up again!

5) Frost the sides—big, rustic swirls are easy to make look good

6) Frost the top, then slide out the parchment

7) Top with fresh raspberries or chocolate shaved with a peeler or sprinkles—or nothing

2 ways to fancy up ice cream

After-dinner drink and dessert in one. And the most forgiving way to make a hot, caramelly sauce, mashed up with banana (or whatever soft fruit you like).

SERVES 4

High-quality vanilla ice cream

4 teaspoons ground espresso coffee (or instant espresso powder such as Medaglia d'Oro)

¼ cup (60ml) Scotch or bourbon

GELATO SPAZZACAMINO
from marcella hazan

1   With an ice cream scoop or spoon, add a scoop or two of ice cream into each of four bowls.

2   Sprinkle 1 teaspoon ground espresso over each scoop, then pour enough Scotch into each bowl to pool at the bottom, about 1 tablespoon each. Serve immediately.

SERVES 6

¼ cup (60g) unsalted butter

½ cup (100g) lightly packed light brown sugar

¼ cup (60ml) whole milk

¼ cup (60ml) heavy cream

Large pinch of flaky sea salt

1 small ripe banana, mashed well with a fork

BANANA BUTTERSCOTCH
from ravneet gill

1 In a saucepan over medium heat, melt the butter, then whisk in the sugar to combine. Add the milk, cream, and salt and bring to a boil, then immediately turn down the heat to a gentle simmer until thickened enough to coat the back of a spoon, about 5 minutes.

2 Add mashed banana to taste. If you want it perfectly smooth, pour through a fine-mesh strainer into a heatproof serving bowl (or buzz with an immersion blender in the pot). Spoon over ice cream (maybe with sliced ripe bananas and cocoa nibs).

the basics

where to put everything

These recommendations are both to help your ingredients last longer and to help you find (and cook with) them without wasting a thing.

by the stove:

- pinch bowl of your favorite salt for seasoning
- pepper grinder
- modest amounts of your go-to cooking oils

on the counter:

- tomatoes (upside down to prevent moisture loss through the stem)
- bananas
- avocados
- any other fruit you want to eat at room temperature
- hard squashes
- bread you want to eat fresh (and quickly—stick the rest in the freezer  p. 250)

in a pantry drawer or cabinet:

- potatoes
- onions and garlic (not with your potatoes or they'll turn on you faster)
- spices (bonus if they're in a drawer or container you can pull out, labeled on top, and organized alphabetically)
- everything canned
- dry grains and pastas and beans
- ice cream sandwiches (JUST KIDDING—if you're still reading, that little joke's for you)
- everything else from the not-freezing and not-misty parts of the grocery store (check labels to see what should relocate to the fridge after opening)

in the front of the fridge (where you won't miss them):

- anything that needs to be used soonest: berries, delicate lettuces, fresh fish, or raw meats (well-wrapped so they don't drip)

in the back of the fridge (the coldest part):

- eggs
- milk you won't use up soon
- anything else that you want to keep extra-cold (beer?)

in the fridge crisper drawers:

- any produce that wasn't stored elsewhere (tip: put the things that need to be used up fastest in a certain area and closer to the front so you don't forget about them)

in the fridge door (the warmest part):

- herbs standing up in jars with a little water 🥄 p. 133
- condiments whose salt, acid, and/ or sugar preserve them for a very long time (hot sauce, mustard, jams, olives, capers)
- technically, not milk and other things that spoil (but it's fine if you go through them pretty quickly)

in the freezer, not necessarily all at once (see page 250 for freezing and thawing tips):

- ice
- ice cream!
- frozen fruits and vegetables, for quick meals and your smoothie library 🥄 p. 28
- whole-grain flours, unless you'll go through them within a month
- nuts and seeds, unless you'll go through them within 3 months

- bread for toasting, sliced while it's still very fresh
- stock 🥄 p. 81
- soups and other saucy leftovers
- bread, cookie, and pie dough
- baked cakes and brownies
- back-up butter (wrapped in foil or a freezer bag—the package alone will let freezer smells in)

- leftover egg yolks, when a recipe called for the whites (and vice versa)
- citrus juice and zest
- ginger (makes it easier to grate!)
- bananas (whole is fine for banana bread, or sliced for milkshakes 🥄 p. 220)

- grapes and kiwi, for snacking (delicious!)
- cooked grains, like farro and rice
- fresh tomatoes, if you'll be using them for sauce later (they'll be extra juicy)

how to befriend your freezer

The freezer is an ally to us home cooks—a magical box that keeps our ingredients and leftovers (almost) locked in time. Here's pretty much all you need to know:

- Freeze everything in a completely sealed container or freezer bag, squeezing out extra air.

- Label everything with the date and what it is (I use painter's tape and a Sharpie). You think you'll remember when that cup of chicken stock is from—I promise you won't.

- Leave an inch (2.5cm) or so of space clear at the top of the container—liquids expand (and, if given no other choice, explode) when frozen.

- No matter what the recipe recommends, the sooner you can get things out of the freezer, the better. Super long stays lead to lost flavor and texture.

- The easiest way to thaw frozen food is to move it to the fridge overnight (unless it's something big like a turkey—those honkers need days). But if you're in a hurry, put well-sealed packages in a bowl of cool water, leaving the faucet running the faintest trickle to keep the water in the bowl moving. Or get to know the "defrost" setting on your microwave.

- See page 249 for a list of ingredients and dishes that freeze especially well.

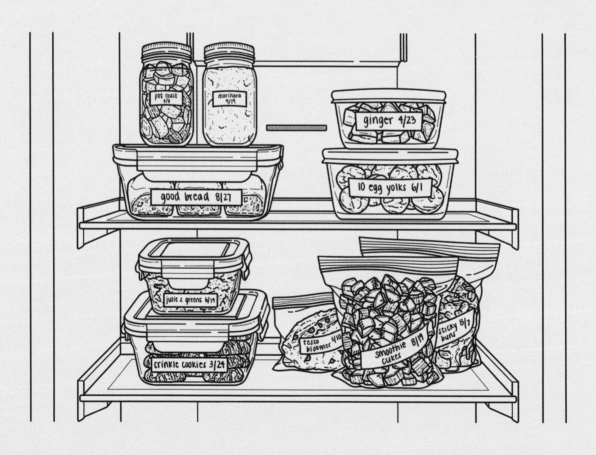

14 essential tools (& the full list to cook everything in this book)

If you have all of the equipment on the next three pages, you can make everything in this book (and so much more). And you can make much of it with just the irreplaceable tools on this page.

Don't feel like you need to buy everything at once—start here and build out as needed, depending on what type of cooking you'd most like to do. Restaurant supply stores are great places to stock up on basics inexpensively (and we carry pretty much everything you see here in the Food52 Shop, too).

14 essential tools

1   **Measuring spoons** (narrow ones fit better in spice jars!)

2   **Dry measuring cups**

3   **Liquid measuring cup**

4   **Large cutting board, preferably wooden**

5   **Chef's knife** (or some people prefer a Santoku or small cleaver—whatever feels good in your hand)

6   **Kitchen towels**

7   **Wooden spoon**

8   **Silicone spatula**

9   **Can opener** (don't try to hack this)

10 **12-inch (30cm) cast-iron skillet**

11 **10-inch (25cm) nontoxic nonstick skillet**

12 **4- to 5-quart (3.8 to 4.7L) Dutch oven or other heavy, lidded pot**

13 **Nested mixing bowl set** (the shallow metal ones from restaurant supply stores are perfect)

14 **Half sheet pan** (or two; the smaller jelly-roll size is fine for smaller households)

cooking utensils:

15 **Wide spatula** (you might want a nonmetal version for using in nonstick pans)

16 **Large balloon whisk** (for casual jobs, a fork is fine)

17 **Tongs**

18 **Good, protective oven mitts**

prep tools:

19 **Large colander**

20 **Pepper grinder**

21 **Microplane**

22 **Paring knife**

23 **Serrated bread knife**

24 **Kitchen scissors** (the kind that comes apart for washing)

25 **Box grater**

26 **Immersion blender** (aka stick blender)

27 **Vegetable peeler**

28 **Knife sharpener** (or find a local shop or butcher who will do it for you)

for storage:

29 **Reusable beeswax wrap**

30 **Reusable lidded containers and Mason jars**

31 **Ice cube tray**

for cooking lots of vegetables:

32 **Salad spinner**

33 **Vegetable scrubby brush**

to cook meat with confidence:

34 **Instant-read thermometer**

35 **Kitchen twine**

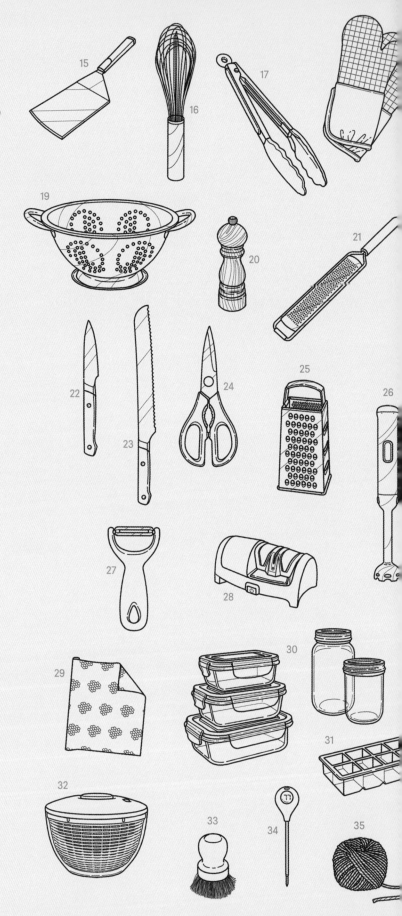

if you like baking:

36 **Digital scale** (better baked goods and less cleanup!)

37 **Oven thermometer**

38 **8-inch (20cm) square pan**

39 **8½ by 4½-inch (21 by 11cm) loaf pan**

40 **9 by 13-inch (23 by 33cm) metal cake pan**

41 **Toothpicks** (or long dry noodles)

42 **Two 8-inch (20cm) round metal cake pans** (or one that's at least 3 inches/7.5cm deep)

43 **Two wire cooling racks**

44 **Butter warmer or other small pot**

45 **Parchment paper** (good news: you can wipe it off and reuse it)

random, not-strictly-necessary things you will use a lot if you have them:

46 **Fine-mesh strainer** (a colander lined with a clean kitchen towel is a decent hack, but this is also handy for blanching ✤ p. 101 and not burning yourself when you drop in your potatoes ✤ p. 164)

47 **Mortar and pestle** (you can hack it ✤ p. 59, but this will grind finer and give you more control—and you can make pesto and garlicky dressings right in it)

48 **Ladle** (heatproof measuring cups work, too)

49 **Quarter sheet pans** (bigger ones do the same thing, but these are handy for small batches of toast or leftovers)

50 **Bench scraper** (for scooping up big chopped piles and scraping up messes fast)

51 **Dish scraper** (a not-metal spatula also works, but this will do the job fast and cheap)

52 **Small offset spatula** (a table knife or the back of a spoon can take over, but this is easier to manipulate)

HOW TO
measure everything

The comfier you are with cooking, the more you'll probably eyeball amounts, but there is so much to be learned and discovered from following recipes to a T, even for the most experienced cooks. Knowing how to use your measuring spoons and cups is key. (Oh, and I'll plug one more time that an inexpensive digital scale means fewer dishes and more consistently great cookies and cakes—see how easy they are to use on page 215.)

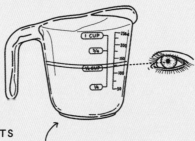

MEASURING LIQUID INGREDIENTS

- Pour into a liquid measuring cup on a level surface and check at eye level.

- If you want to be a scientist, read at the bottom of the U-shaped meniscus (but in most recipes it won't matter much).

- In a pinch, you can use dry measuring cups for measuring liquids, too—just be careful not to spill.

MEASURING DRY (OR STICKY) INGREDIENTS

- Scoop up the ingredient into a dry measuring cup or spoon (for more tips on flour and other tricky powders, see page 215).

- Scrape something flat, like the back of a table knife, over the top to level (especially important for leaveners like baking soda, baking powder, and yeast, and powerful spices).

- For sticky stuff, scrape it all out with a silicone spatula or your finger (and really sticky stuff like honey will come out easier if you oil the cup first).

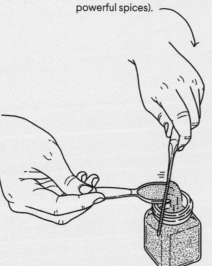

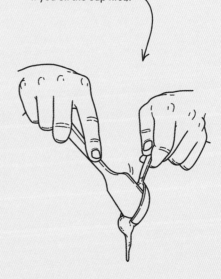

knife safety 101

The most important rule in knife safety is to respect that you are holding something that can unlock much of cooking to you—and can do serious damage (great power, great responsibility). Dull knife or sharp, if you're distracted or moving too fast, you can get cuts that really get in the way of making dinner.

While I'm all for rule-breaking in most parts of cooking, the sharp—and hot—object rules that keep order and safety in restaurant kitchens (and in Girl Scouts) work great at home, too.

- The safest place to store sharp knives is on a magnetic knife rack (easy to install on the wall—promise) or in a knife block, and definitely not loose in a general tool drawer.

- Hand-wash them—the dishwasher can dull and warp.

- Don't leave sharp knives in the sink or other places people might not see them (the water can also rust the blades and warp wooden handles).

- Keep the blade pointing down at your side as you walk.

- If you have to walk behind someone while holding a sharp (or hot) object, warn them with plenty of notice that you're coming through and to stay put (in culinary school, we said "knife behind" or "hot behind"—fun to say at home, too).

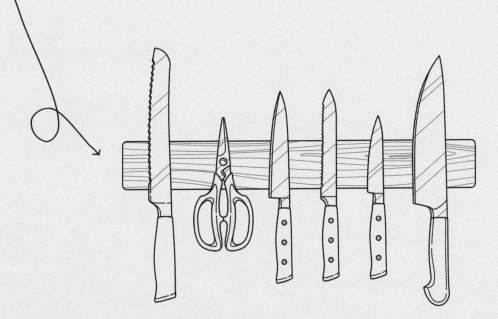

HOW TO
deal with onions

There are lots of ways to cut an onion for different shapes and textures—even lots of ways to *chop* an onion to come up with roughly a ½-inch (1.3cm) dice. This is the way I use most often, but ask people how they do it the next time you cook with them and you might discover your new favorite.

Quick note: If you use the same cutting board for onions and fruit, your fruit will taste like onions, even after washing—consider having a separate cutting board just for garlic and onions.

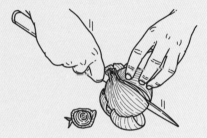

1) Trim just the hairy root, then cut in half through the cut end

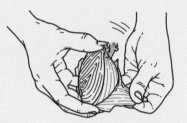

2) Peel away all papery skin

3) Trim the dry tip on the stem ends

TO SLICE:

1) Slice as thin or thick as you want, crosswise in half-moons or radially in wedges

TO CHOP:

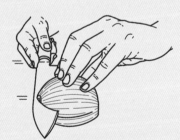

1) Carefully make horizontal cuts, leaving the root end intact to hold everything together

2) Make vertical cuts toward the root, again leaving the root intact

3) Make vertical cuts crosswise to shear off rows of chopped onion

HOW TO
deal with garlic

Much like onions, there are so many ways to prep garlic, and each brings out a slightly different flavor. Grating, for example, is a quick way to make a garlic paste, but crushes the cells and creates the sharpest, most pungent flavor. You probably want to use grated garlic more sparingly than garlic that's been smashed, sliced, minced, or even mashed to a paste, and the tinier it is, the faster it will cook.

Same quick note as on page 256: If you don't want garlicky fruit, consider having a separate cutting board just for garlic and onions.

1) Pull off cloves from the head

TO SLICE OR GRATE:

2) If you need the clove intact, twist the papery skin to loosen and peel away

3a) Trim the tough dry nub and slice crosswise or lengthwise

3b) Or grate on a Microplane, avoiding the nub

TO SMASH, MINCE, OR MASH TO A PASTE:

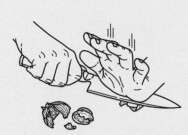

1) If you don't need the clove intact, smash it under the side of your knife—the peel will fall away

2) To mince, rock the knife through till it's as fine as you like

3) Then, for a paste, sprinkle salt on top and scrape against the cutting board with the side of your knife

HOW TO
deal with herbs

Herbs bring so much flavor and life to cooking but can be a little picky about how they're handled (unless you're using them in whole sprigs, like stuffing in a roast chicken or simmering in a pot of beans—both very handy ways to use up the rest of the bunch). Here's how to treat them as they want to be treated.

WASHING (AND, IMPORTANTLY, DRYING)

If they don't feel gritty, a rinse and good pat dry with a clean towel is fine. To wash them well, see page 185. To trick them into staying fresh longer, see page 133.

SOFT HERBS (CILANTRO, MINT, DILL, PARSLEY, TARRAGON, BASIL)

1) Any soft parts of the stems are edible...

2)...so the amount you pluck off is mostly about what texture you prefer

HARDY HERBS (ROSEMARY AND THYME)

3) But these hard stems have to go

4) grab the thickest end of the stem and slide the leaves off—wherever it naturally breaks, the stem is tender enough to eat

TO CHOP OR MINCE ANY HERB:

1) Make sure they're nice and dry

2) Gather a pile of leaves under your nondominant hand, forming a claw to protect your fingers

3a) Chop with your other hand, sliding your knife down and away from you

3b) For basil or other big leaves, it helps to stack the leaves, roll them up, and slice into ribbons

4) With your nondominant hand lightly resting on the dull back side of the blade as a balance, rock your knife up and down through the pile

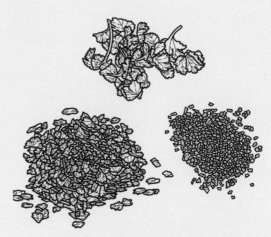

5) Chop is generally rougher than mince, though it's all relative—so you decide what looks good to you

HOW TO
deal with ginger

There are all sorts of tricks for easy access to the sweet, fiery punch of fresh ginger, for brothy soups (page 114), creamy porridges (page 166), and more. And if you have extra, freeze it (page 250)—it will be even easier to grate.

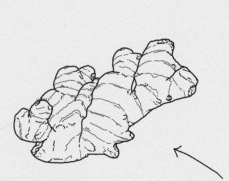

1) Choose hunks of ginger that don't look shriveled, with fewer little knobs and more big, meaty sections

2) (Andrea Nguyen cuts the tiny knobs off to save for boiling into ginger tea, rather than peeling around them)

3) Peel with the tip of a spoon, scraping back toward you

Don't stress about getting it all (some chefs, like Anita Jaisinghani and Zoe Adjonyoh don't peel at all)

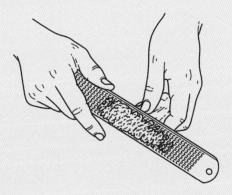

4a) Slice, chop, or mince as fine as you like . . .

4b) . . . or carefully grate it for pulp that leaves all the fibers behind

HOW TO
deal with nuts

When nuts are good and toasted, they have a deep flavor and snap—you can tell they are done when they smell great and look golden through the middle when you break a couple open. Here are a few ways to get there.

1a) Most even/least burning: Toast whole, shelled nuts in the oven at 325°F (165°C) on a sheet pan, checking every few minutes and shaking the pan so they cook evenly (they should take 8 to 12 minutes)

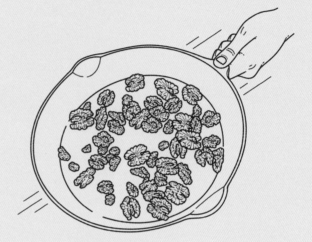

OR

1b) Toast in a dry skillet over medium heat, shaking frequently and vigilantly—these are easier to burn

THEN

2) Chop them as rough or fine as you want (you can toast them after chopping, but the fine bits burn more easily that way)

mostly love doing the dishes

I am part of the especially nerdy faction of home cooks who find doing the dishes relaxing—and you can, too! (Or work out a deal with your housemates so someone else does the dishes when you cook.)

We all have our own favorite methods for working through a full sink, informed by trial and error and intuition—here's mine:

- Scrape and rinse all dishes soon after you're done with them, so food has less of a chance to become one with the plate.

- Fill any really grubby ones with hot, soapy water to soak, and pile silverware into a glass or bowl to soak, too.

- When you're ready to wash them all, put on a podcast or good playlist.

- If you have a dishwasher, great! Load it up, and leave out anything wooden or cast iron 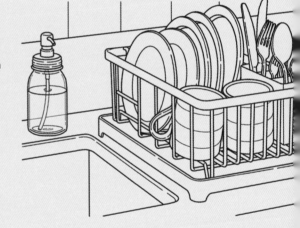 p. 263, sharp knives, and anything else not sold as dishwasher-safe. I leave out big bowls and pans, too, because they crowd out everything else.

- For everything else, get a sponge with one scrubby side really soapy with dish soap (my favorite is Sal Suds from Dr. Bronner's).

- Scrub the insides and outsides of all the dishes and stack them up, still soapy, by the sink.

- Bonus points if you save oily ones till the end, because the oil might resist the soap and transfer onto other dishes.

- Rinse them all with hot water in one go and stack them carefully, upside down so the water can run out, in a dish rack or on clean kitchen towels on the counter.

- For really pesky sticky stuff, like egg yolk or melted cheese, soak if needed, then use a plastic dish scraper or a nonmetal spatula to scrape off as much as you can before washing, so you grub up the sponge as little as possible.

- Wipe down the counter and feel accomplished.

HOW TO DEAL WITH BURNT POTS

Everybody burns pots now and again. When you do, soak them until you can face them and survey the damage. Then, try these tips—they almost always work.

- Sometimes, especially for sugary substances, boiling water in the sticky pot and then carefully pouring it down the sink drain can free the stuck-on bits (just don't do this with cast iron unless it's enameled or you might wash away some of the nonstick seasoning—more on this below).

- Try a mild abrasive, like baking soda or coarse salt, scrubbing with a wet sponge (some swear by scrubbing salt around with a halved lemon).

- If those don't work, try a chemical solvent like Bar Keepers Friend.

- Soak and repeat as needed, but usually you only have to do one or two of these.

HOW TO TAKE CARE OF CAST IRON (IT'S WAY EASIER THAN YOU THINK)

If you buy a pre-seasoned cast-iron pan, as most are sold these days, all you have to do to maintain its nonstick seasoning is not mess it up, which is surprisingly easy.

- Cook in it often, especially with fats—they'll keep seasoning the pan and making it more nonstick.

- If you cooked something not very perishable in oil (like toast or nuts) and it didn't leave anything sticky behind, you can just wipe it out well with a clean kitchen towel (that you don't mind staining with black smudges) or paper towel.

- If you cooked something you want to wash out with hot water and dish soap—like smash burgers or something saucy—that's actually okay!

- Wash as you would other dishes, lightly scrubbing with a sponge (no harsh chemicals or abrasives like steel wool—those will mess with the seasoning).

- Never soak the pan in the sink or leave it to dry in a rack or it will rust—wipe it dry with a towel (that you don't mind staining) and put it on the stovetop over high heat to dry.

- Don't walk away—when the pan is dry and starting to smoke, turn off the heat (and turn on the fan).

- With oven mitts, slide the pan to a cool burner.

- While it's still hot, put in a few drops of neutral oil, and carefully wipe a very thin coat all over the pan with a dry towel, then leave to cool.

- To store once it's cool, stack with a towel for buffer from other pans.

- Make sure any housemates know the rules!

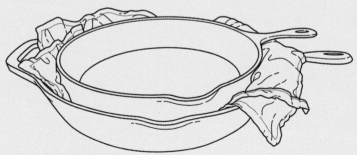

IDEAS IN FOOD — GREAT RECIPES and WHY THEY WORK — AKI KAMOZAWA and H. ALEXANDER TALBOT

RUSS PARSONS — how to pick a peach — The Search for Flavor from Farm to Table

Russ Parsons — How to Read a French Fry — and Other Stories of Intriguing Kitchen Science

BRAVETART — ICONIC AMERICAN DESSERTS — STELLA PARKS

THE FLAVOR EQUATION — Sharma

THE CAKE BIBLE — ROSE LEVY BERANBAUM

SALT FAT ACID HEAT — SAMIN NOSRAT

ROBERT L. WOLKE — WHAT EINSTEIN TOLD HIS COOK

THE FOOD LAB — J. KENJI LÓPEZ-ALT — Better Home Cooking Through Science

ON FOOD AND COOKING — HAROLD McGEE

CookWise — Shirley O. Corriher

BakeWise — The Hows, and Whys of Successful Baking — SHIRLEY O. CORRIHER

further reading & cooking

I hope this book has given you a hundred or so leads on new cookbooks to read and authors to follow, listed in the recipes' introductions.

And if you love understanding *why* recipes work as much as I do, check out the books that I keep close by for reference on my favorite shelves.

Ideas in Food by Aki Kamozawa & H. Alexander Talbot

How to Read a French Fry and *How to Pick a Peach* by Russ Parsons

BraveTart by Stella Parks

The Flavor Equation by Nik Sharma

The Cake Bible and other baking bibles by Rose Levy Beranbaum

Salt Fat Acid Heat by Samin Nosrat

What Einstein Told His Cook (and its sequels) by Robert L. Wolke

The Food Lab by J. Kenji López-Alt

On Food and Cooking by Harold McGee

CookWise and *BakeWise* by Shirley Corriher

thank-yous

To all the geniuses, both in this book and on Food52.

To Amanda Hesser, whose brilliant idea started this whole thing, and Merrill Stubbs, for a decade of generosity, encouragement, and cackles.

To my daughter, Mari, for changing everything and giving me so many more reasons to love being in the kitchen. To my husband-slash-cameraperson, Mike, the Vern to my Ernest, for carrying us through and making me laugh for sixteen years (and counting). To my brother, Billy, for being every book's first editor and my cooking buddy ever since the bad pasta salad rut of the late '90s.

To my parents, Susan and Allen Miglore, for teaching me how to cook both with recipes and without, respectively, and letting me find my own way out of picky eating (it worked). To my endlessly kind father- and mother-in-law, Art and Tuny Dunkley, without whose support this book would still be an untouched spreadsheet from 2019. To Desiree Garibaldi and Ronda Fletcher, for taking such good care of our daughter, and us.

To my late grandmother, Grace Cowan, and the biscuits and gravy line of the Cowan family. To my late grandparents, Mike and Thann Miglore, and the rest of the deep-dish Miglores. To my second family, Dan, Erin, Riley, and Josh Dunkley, for appreciating a good bacon hack as much as I do.

To everyone at Ten Speed Press: Julie Bennett, Emma Campion, Kim Keller, Mari Gill, Serena Sigona, Zoey Brandt, Faith Hague, Kathy Brock, Nick Patton, Tammy White, David Hawk, and Stephanie Davis, for being the best partners, three books deep, and especially to this book's designer Lizzie Allen, for twisting the Rubik's Cube of this concept with me over and over and bringing it to life. To Food52's agents, Binky Urban and Kari Stuart—how did we ever do this without you?

To our superhuman photo team: James Ransom, Alexis Anthony, Anna Billingskog, Allison Bruns Buford, Samantha Seneviratne, Amanda Widis, Molly FitzSimons, Alya Hameedi, Townsend Smith, César Pérez Medero, William Johnson, Danielle Curtis-Williams, and Eddie Barrera—you made miracles. To our dream illustrator Eliana Rodgers, who made the last of so many big question marks on this project feel joyful and effortless.

To Emily Hanhan, Emily Stephenson, Caroline Lange, and Coral Lee, for tracking down the research and recipes that anchor this book. To Suzanne D'Amato for putting the idea for this book into the ether. To my column editors at Food52, most recently Eric Kim, Emma Laperruque, and Margaret Eby, for teaching me so much about writing, and special thanks to Eric for making the title and intro to this book so much better. To Stacey Rivera and Brinda Ayer, for years of advice connecting the dots with the rest of the Food52 universe, and Elizabeth Spiridakis Olson, for joining us at just the right time to bring new life to the cover. To Gabriella Mangino, Alik Barsoumian, Ayanna Long, Rob Strype, Wonbo Woo, Grant Melton, and Alan Capriles for helping this nightshift writer figure out how to act on YouTube, and Coral Lee, Amy Shuster, Emily Hanhan, and Harry Sultan for joining brains to turn it all into a podcast every week.

To our indefatigable recipe testers Stephanie Bourgeois, Kate Knapp, Anna Francese Gass, and Susan Streit Sherman, and the Food52 Cookbook and Baking Clubs for your invaluable feedback (I fixed the salt for you!). To Ali Slagle and CB Owens, for the most thoughtful proofreading on virtually every book since Genius the First.

To my colleagues and mentors who were so generous with their time and ideas: Andrea Nguyen, Maria Speck, Charlotte Druckman, Matt Sartwell, the late Nach Waxman, Jessie Sheehan, Naomi Duguid, Eugenia Bone, Celia Sack, Naz Deravian, Aliya LeeKong, Aglaia Kremezi, Carlos Olaechea, Peter Berley, Urvashi Pitre, Sarit Packer, Itamar Srulovich, Raquel Pelzel, Rose Levy Beranbaum, Nik Sharma, Alex Raij, Peter Miller, Anna Jones, Bill Smith, Russ Parsons, Molly Stevens, Victoria Granof, Ian Knauer, J. Kenji López-Alt, Louisa Shafia, Julia Bainbridge, Julia Turshen, Heidi Swanson, Daniela Galarza, Hillary and Angela Fong, Lauren Dowling, and Anita Shepherd.

And, especially, to the ever-growing community who still makes Food52 the most welcoming corner of the internet. Swapping ideas with you all is the highlight of my work, and this book would not exist without you.

genius tipsters

Thank you to the countless members of the decade-long Genius Recipes focus group, happening every day on Food52, YouTube, Facebook, and Instagram and in my inbox at genius@food52.com. You have changed the way I cook. These are the names—some real, some Food52 or YouTube avatars—of the people whose smart tips appear in this book.

A G	Eric Kim	Louise @ Using Mainly Spoons
Adam Janofsky	Erica T.	Lune
Alexandra Stafford	Gabriella Mangino	maci B.
Ali Slagle	hardlikearmour	Marian Bull
April McGreger	healthierkitchen	mikeficus
Brette Warshaw	Heather G.	mrslarkin
Brinda Ayer	Heidi Reinberg	Patrick Moynihan
Burton D.	Jenny Meier	Raquel Pelzel
Caroline Lange	Julianne Bell	Sally Baker
Catherine Newman	Kari Johnson	Sandra E.
Cheryl D.	Kelsey Burrow	Sarah Jampel
Coral Lee	Kenzi Wilbur	Sharon Sone
drbabs	Kevin G.	Tere
Emily Hanhan	Kristy Mucci	violist
Emily Nunn	Lindsay-Jean Hard	William S.
Emily Stephenson	linzarella	Wonbo Woo

index

Some of the recipes in this work first appeared on the Food52 website.

Typeface: Larsseit by Type Dynamic

Library of Congress Cataloging-in-Publication Data

Names: Miglore, Kristen, author. | Ransom, James (Photographer), photographer.
Title: Food52 simply genius: recipes for beginners, busy cooks & curious people / Kristen Miglore; photography by James Ransom.
Other titles: Food 52 simply genius | Food52.
Description: First editon. | California: Ten Speed Press, [2022] | Series: Food52 works | Includes index.
Identifiers: LCCN 2021038258 (print) | LCCN 2021038259 (ebook) | ISBN 9780399582943 (hardcover) | ISBN 9780399582950 (ebook)
Subjects: LCSH: Cooking. | LCGFT: Cookbooks.
Classification: LCC TX714 .M5353 2022 (print) | LCC TX714 (ebook) | DDC 641.5—dc23
LC record available at https://lccn.loc.gov/2021038258
LC ebook record available at https://lccn.loc.gov/2021038259

Hardcover ISBN: 978-0-399-58294-3
eBook ISBN: 978-0-399-58295-0

Printed in China

Editor: Julie Bennett | Production editor: Kim Keller | Editorial assistant: Zoey Brandt
Designer: Lizzie Allen | Art director: Emma Campion | Production designers: Mari Gill and Faith Hague
Production manager: Serena Sigona
Prepress color manager: Nick Patton
Food stylists: Anna Billingskog and Samantha Seneviratne
Prop stylists: Amanda Widis, Molly FitzSimons, and Alya Hameedi
Photo retoucher: Tammy White
Copyeditor: Amy Kovalski | Proofreaders: Kathy Brock, Ali Slagle, and CB Owens | Indexer: Ken DellaPenta
Publicist: David Hawk | Marketer: Stephanie Davis

10 9 8 7 6 5 4 3 2 1

First Edition